MW00611258

 O R E G O N

LODGE
COOKING

Recipes & Memories from Summers at Lake Creek

J U L I   T A N T U M

OREGON LODGE COOKING:
Recipes & Memories from Summers at Lake Creek

Copyright © 2015 by Juli Tantum.

All rights reserved, including the right of
reproduction in whole or in part in any form.

www.OregonLodgeCooking.com

Library of Congress Control Number: 2015905954

ISBN: 978-0-9861798-0-8 (print),
978-0-9861798-1-5 (ebook)

Cover photos by Robert Swingle
Book design by Shannon Bodie,
BookWiseDesign.com

Manufactured in the United States of America.
First edition, June 2015

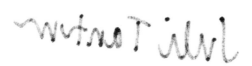

FOR ROBLAY

"I could tell what day it was by what was for dinner."

— Sally Follen

CONTENTS

Glazed Carrots
Fresh Fruit with Cookies

    Oatmeal Scotchies

    Lemon Bars

    Chocolate Chip Cookies

    Blanche's Snickerdoodles

    Brownies

Popovers
Fruit Plate with "Caribbean" Fruit Sauce
Prime Rib
Oven-Browned Potato Wedges
Green Beans
Carrot Cake with Cream Cheese Icing

Hard Cornbread
Green Salad with Tavern Vinaigrette
Roast Leg of Lamb
Lake Creek Mint Sauce
Curried Rice
White Rice with Gravy
Sautéed Carrots, Celery & Onions
Blueberry Buckle

Sixty Minute Rolls
Corn Chowder
Honey-Mustard Glazed Ham
Raisin Sauce
Dijon Sauce
Scalloped Potatoes
Broccoli with Parmesan
Banana Cream Pie

Alternate Thursday Menu

Sixty Minute Rolls or Banana Bread
Lake Creek Lodge Salad
Roast Turkey
Cornbread Stuffing
Gravy
Mashed Potatoes
Broccoli with Parmesan
Chocolate Brownie Pie
No-Fail Pie Crust

Pitch Boats

Cinnamon Sticky Buns
Crunchy Cabbage Salad
Grilled Salmon with Tartar Sauce
Walla Walla Onion-Rice Casserole
Ice Cream Sundaes with Butterscotch Sauce
    & "Lake Creek" Chocolate Sauce

Departure

Lake Creek Lodge Raisin Bread
Buttermilk Pancakes
Cornmeal Battercakes
Sourdough Pancakes
Morning Glory Muffins
Old Fashioned Blueberry Muffins
Coffee Cake

INTRODUCTION

THE DINNER BELL RANG EVERY SUMMER EVENING AT Lake Creek Lodge, summoning guests to the deck for another delicious meal. This book is a tribute to a specific lodge, nestled amid the mountains and streams of central Oregon. But it could be familiar to every family who has filled their station wagon and headed off on a lodge vacation. If you visited Lake Creek Lodge between 1940 and 1990, then the stories and recipes in this book will be familiar. Even if you weren't a guest during those years, the food represents lodge cooking during that era. And if you cook the recipes, the aromas that fill your kitchen will transport you back to those times — to an outdoor deck on a warm summer evening and a knotty-pine paneled dining room on a crisp mountain morning.

Lake Creek Lodge favorites included the traditional layered Ice Cream Cake with "Lake Creek" Chocolate Sauce drizzled over top, which guests looked forward to all year; the Creamy Polenta with melted cheese, which perfectly complimented Bud's sizzling Grilled New York Steaks; and the stacks of steaming Cornmeal Battercakes that filled the warm lodge dining room with the scent of corn and pancakes for early morning breakfasts. The daily menus seldom varied over the years. Guests could depend on the same wonderfully fresh, homemade food each summer.

Many of the original handwritten and hand-typed recipes were found in a black metal recipe box years after the main cook had retired. Some of the yellowed recipe cards had very specific lists of ingredients and others had very few. Often the instructions were sparse and lacking in measurements or cooking times. But that was because the cooks in the Lake Creek Lodge kitchen were preparing the same dishes multiple times each summer, and they had most of them committed to memory. That was part of the charm and allure of Lake Creek Lodge and other lodges of its time: amid a quickly changing world, it was an oasis of simplicity that stayed true to its traditions. There was comfort in knowing that this part of life didn't change, and that it was possible to leave behind bustling cities, calendars and obligations to be among the company of friends and family.

For many, the sound of the dinner bell brings back the summertime memories. Although new cabins have been built, and the lodge now has Wi-Fi and a different meal plan, Lake Creek's sense of tradition remains.

Before I was old enough to swim in the pond, my family was making an annual trip to Lake Creek Lodge, carrying on the traditions created by earlier families. Today, guests from Oregon, California, Washington, and beyond still meet up at our favorite place. We pick up where we left off each summer, even if our only communication during the rest of the year is a holiday card. Lake Creek Lodge is a small resort with cabins surrounding a main lodge, a tennis court, a pool, a trout-stocked pond, and the eponymous Lake Creek running through the wooded property.

A few summers ago, I began gathering recipes with the help of former employees and fellow guests. Our longtime chef Blanche Williams had retired, previous owner Velda Brust had just passed away, and with both of them went many of the menus that guests had grown up with during their summertime vacations. Menus that were written each morning on the chalkboard that hung in the kitchen.

I sifted through recipes while sitting on cabin porches by the creek. Family members and friends walked by on their way to the pool or tennis court and offered their own renditions of the food served at the lodge. Stories began to flow. And it turned out there were a lot of them. One moonlit evening a group of us gathered inside the cozy living room of Cabin 5, telling stories and laughing until midnight. As we walked outside to the gurgling sound of the creek, we realized that food was the tangible part of our past that made Lake Creek Lodge so magical.

But Lake Creek Lodge dinners were about more than just the recipes. The food brought all of us together each night, but the menus weren't particularly fancy (just like our cabins). The important part was the time we spent together growing up along mint-lined Lake Creek.

1940's meal inside the lodge dining room

The pages that follow contain many of the old recipes. But I've added instructions and made small changes where necessary. I relied on the memories of guests and former staff for instructions on how, for example, the Oven-Fried Chicken got its crispy coating, or how the Cinnamon Sticky Buns came out the size of small dinner rolls. For recipes that were vague, I did some detective work, such as uncovering the secret ingredient in "Caribbean" Fruit Sauce (orange liqueur), or determining how much was "a handful" of raisins in Lake Creek Lodge Raisin Bread (one cup). Some of the older recipes were from wartime days and called for oleo, another word for margarine, so in those cases I've substituted butter. (Even when ingredients were scarce due to wartime rationing, the resourceful owner Roblay somehow got a hold of butter and parceled it out carefully to guests). Many recipes made large quantities to serve a full deck of lodge guests. In those instances, I halved or quartered recipes so they are better suited to a family.

These menus are largely from the earlier era in the kitchen. Over the years they evolved slowly, but they remained traditional "meat-and-potato" meals accompanied by various side dishes. The classic dishes endured because they were perfect after the long hikes, swims and horse back rides that filled Lake Creek days. The decades since have brought change, but the original menus are what shaped the first 50 years of our Lake Creek Lodge experiences.

The recipes speak for themselves — the food was good and simple, as lodge cooking is meant to be. And they translate well to the home kitchen so you can easily re-create the traditional dinners with family and friends, and re-live your own Lake Creek Lodge memories.

HISTORY OF
LAKE CREEK LODGE

LAKE CREEK LODGE IS LOCATED IN THE CASCADES REGION of Central Oregon, near a small mountain town called Camp Sherman. The town is centered around a general store and tiny post office. Down the road there is an elementary school, a restaurant, and campgrounds. Along the nearby Metolius River there are cabins (some seasonal and others year-round), and a few small resorts. And slightly further out are homes scattered in meadows and along the river. The nearest large community is the town of Sisters, which earned its name in 1888 from the looming Three Sisters mountains. Sisters has retained a charming cowboy feeling in the façade of the buildings lining the main street and the wide ranches near the entrance to town.

The most striking thing about Lake Creek Lodge is the beauty of its surroundings, especially to out-of-town guests: The majestic snow-capped mountains rising above meadows dotted with colorful wildflowers, pristine streams and icy-cold rivers, forested trails, and expanses of ranchland with grazing horses and cattle.

For such a small resort, the history behind Lake Creek Lodge is a bit elaborate. Fortunately many of the details were preserved in writing, and photographs help complete the stories remembered by guests.

It all began around 1921, when Martin and Lena Hansen purchased 80 acres of land and created some tent cabins for rent at Hansen's Resort. By 1924, it was renamed Martin Hansen's Resort on the Metolius. Martin and his family had built cabins, dammed up Lake Creek for swimming, built two foot bridges and a lodge with a dining room. They also had horses for saddle or packing. Cabins rented for $1.75 a day, and guests could board their horse for an additional 75 cents. There was a sheep-pasture golf course across the road (the current site of the Metolius Meadows). It was said that each cabin was equipped with one electric light that was strung from the cabins to the main lodge. So when Martin went to bed, so did everybody else since he turned off the switch and all the property went dark!

Meanwhile in San Francisco at the time, a spunky 19 year-old woman named Roblay had recently moved to the city and worked for a successful firm where she met a dashing man named Bud McMullin. Bud and Roblay married in the 1920's and moved to eastern Oregon to set up a horse ranch.

Bud's sister, the outgoing socialite Mrs. Eliza Gallois, had become a friend of Roblay's in San Francisco before they moved. During a driving trip through Central Oregon in the summer of 1925, Eliza and her husband John purchased property along the Metolius River and arranged to have a large summer home built. Known as the House on Metolius, the Galloises used their home until they sold it in 1947.

Around the time the Galloises were spending summers on the Metolius, Mrs. Bertha Ronalds, a tobacco heiress of the Lorillard Tobacco family and friend of Eliza's, visited them after returning from Paris. Bertha decided she also wanted a summer residence in Oregon and thought the Metolius Valley was the perfect location. She purchased Hansen's Resort along with the meadow opposite it, and chose to build a home and ranch in the Metolius Meadow.

Meanwhile, Bud and Roblay were "horse rustled," and were trying to figure out where they would go after losing all of their horses. Eliza knew that Bertha needed help running her new home and ranch, and suggested that Bud and Roblay apply for the job. Needless to say, they were a perfect match. Bud became the ranch manager, and Roblay became Bertha's companion for horseback rides.

Eventually, Bertha deeded her house, property and the resort to Bud and Roblay. In order to raise enough money to make improvements to the resort, Bud and Roblay sold Bertha's house and property. Over the next four years, Bud and Roblay were busy with construction projects and re-named the resort Lake Creek

Calaveras + Chico Aug. '38

Bud and Roblay riding Calaveras and Chico, August 1938

Lodge. Bud tore down most of the simple cabins and made plans for new ones, which he would build largely on his own. In April of 1937, the *Bend Bulletin* reported the construction of a new lodge and ten deluxe cabins of "rustic type" to be ready by June 1st. A Bend contractor named Henry Nelson was hired to help Bud. The cabins were to fit "unobtrusively into the mountain and forest setting." Each cottage would have two bedrooms, a kitchenette with gas range, dining alcove, shower and toilet. The new lodge would have a beamed ceiling and massive fireplace, with a knotty pine finish. The *Bulletin* went on to describe the bucolic Lake Creek Lodge setting as being a "short distance from the Metolius River, which emerges as giant springs from a point near the base of Black Butte. Nearby are the giant peaks of the Cascade Range, Mt. Jefferson, Mt. Washington, Three-Fingered Jack, and the Three Sisters."

Since Lake Creek was a summer resort, Bud and Roblay would close it down for the winter and move to Palm Springs where they ran a small resort in Indio. They did this for about four years until 1955, when during their drive south Bud suffered a heart attack in Redding and died. Roblay sold the Palm Springs resort and continued to run Lake Creek Lodge with the help of her small, loyal staff.

Ave – took Summer '49

Roblay and Bud, 1949

According to a 1969 article in the *Oregonian*, "Lake Creek Lodge had a dammed creek for swimming, rustic cabins polished till they gleam and a real dinner bell which clangs at 7 p.m. to call residents to dinner in the casual, sprawling lodge… Prices for cottages begin at $36 for two or $13 per person for four or more. Dinner included and breakfast available from 8:30–10 a.m."

In 1974, Roblay sold Lake Creek Lodge to three women, "the Ladies from OSU": Velda Brust, Margaret Lumpkin and Lisa Taubman. Formerly professors at Oregon State (Velda was an athletic coach and taught physical therapy; Margaret taught psychology), the women also owned and operated Camp Tamarack, a girls' camp nearby. They were extraordinary women — educators, published authors, compassionate and caring. Velda ran the day-to-day operations at Lake Creek

Lodge and could be seeing doing everything around the property. During their ownership, the women added insulation and heat to the cabins to turn Lake Creek Lodge into a year-round operation. Diana Pepperling stayed on as manager.

As part of the sale agreement, Roblay had life tenancy in her own cabin adjacent to Lake Creek. "Roblay's Cabin" is now Cabin 11. Her official title was Hostess, and responsibilities included greeting guests and mingling with them at dinner. Roblay's outfits were legendary. During the day she dressed casually in pants, but for dinner (especially in her older age), she went all out. She often wore flamboyant hats and large pieces of Parisian jewelry inherited from Bertha, and her ensembles ranged from full leopard print to white tights decorated with red hearts. Roblay would make the little walk from her cabin to the dining patio, drink in hand and her small frame teetering on heels, with her loyal dog Daisy trailing close behind. She complained about most of the resort changes, but she excelled at her unofficial role and carried it out until she died on August 6, 1998 at the age of 91. In 2003, the women sold the resort to Jeff and Gordon Jones, the current owners.

HOTEL REGISTER

Money, Jewelry and other Valuables must be placed in the Safe in the Office otherwise the Hotel will not be responsible for any loss.

DATE	NAME	STREET ADDRESS	CITY		ROOM NO.	Time of Arrival	Time of Depart.
6/28/49	Mr + Mrs Paul H. Williams	3311 N.E. Couch	Portland	Oregon		4/15/49	6/
6/28/49	Maureen Williams	3311 N.E. Couch	Portland	Oregon		4/19/46	4
6/25/49	Gretchen Graap	4431 N.E. Alameda	Portland	Oregon		9/25/49	4/
6/29/49	Joan Sinton	2550 Divisadero	San Francisco	Calif		6/29/49	7/20
6/29/49	Pam Heaton	2761 Divisadero	San Francisco	Calif.		6/29/49	7/
6/29/49	Jennison Heaton	2761 Divisadero	San Francisco	Calif			
6/28/49	Mr + Mrs Glenn R. Harrison	7031 Colton	Oakland	Cal			
7/1/49	Mr + Mrs Paul R. Collins & daughter Nancy + Mary Collins	705 Canterbury Rd.	San Marino	Calif			
7/1/49	Mr + Mrs Eugene F. Davidson + Nancy Dell	830 NE 70	Portland 14	Oreg.		7/1/49	7/15
7/1/49	Mrs Victor W. Johnson, Mrs Karl Graue Jr.	Tigard, 2429 N.E. Bragee	Oregon, Portland	Oreg.		7/1/49	7/31
7/1/49	Mr + Mrs William J. Oliver + Dane Oliver	277 E. Leone St.	Clark's Green, Scranton	Penna		7/1/49	7/15
7/1/49	Mr + Mrs Ben Hager, Mrs Walter Miller & Family	2832 S.E. Monica	Portland	Ore		7/1/49	7/1
	Mr + Mrs John J. Rogers	2187 University St.	Eugene				
7/3	Mr + Mrs W. J. Collins	7797 Southwest Oldsworth Ht.	Portland				
7/3	Mr + Mrs Fred Seubert and family	3535 S.E. Jameson Road	Beaverton	Ore			
7/3	Mr. & Mrs. Allen Van Duyn and Family	4431 NE Western Dr.	Portland				
	Mr + Mrs A. L. Seubert	Rt 1 Lake Grove, Oregon				Blocked	

DAY 1

SATURDAY

Arrival & Menu

Baking Powder Biscuits
Lake Creek Lodge Salad
Oven-Fried Chicken
Mashed Potatoes with Gravy
Peas with Shallots
Ice Cream Cake with "Lake Creek" Chocolate Sauce

THE FIRST SATURDAY OF A LAKE CREEK VACATION was the best day of summer. Some of us drove 10 hours straight from San Francisco; others had a short drive from Portland. Either way, we'd pull into Lake Creek Lodge's gravel driveway, jump out of the car and take a long, deep breath of the pine-scented air that is only Lake Creek. We had waited all year to be there, and now we had a whole glorious week (or two or three…) stretched out ahead of us.

For months beforehand, this trip was on all of our minds. Holiday cards would end with, "See you at Lake Creek!" And when we were shopping for clothes during the year, we'd find ourselves remarking, "Wouldn't that be good for Lake Creek?" That being said, many guests, especially the mothers, would pack the same plaid skirts and dresses each year since their summertime wardrobes had become part of the tradition. Even in rustic Sisters, we were fashionable on vacation.

"70" Tim · Annette Ryan

We'd check in at the front desk where Roblay would have her big reservation book opened for us to sign, walk through the lodge to check out any changes, and then head to the cabins. The old wooden bridge across the creek was built to accommodate a car, so we'd drive the station wagons across the bridge, park on the lawn in front of our cabins and unpack. Once that bridge became too old for cars it was replaced with a stone pedestrian bridge and now we park in the dirt lot behind the cabins.

As we unpacked, other cars would trickle in and we'd reunite with our old friends. We'd also keep an eye out for first-time families and the prospect of new Lake Creek friends. We moved into our bedrooms and kitchens, carrying bags and groceries up the steps of the impeccable knotty-pine cabins. There was usually just enough time for a quick dip in the pond or a shower before cocktail hour would begin at 6 p.m. In the old days there was a more formal "dress code" of sport coats and ties for men, and skirts for ladies. Children would have pressed sundresses and ironed cotton shirts. Now we still dress up a bit for dinner, but things are more casual.

When Roblay and Bud McMullin first started running Lake Creek Lodge, guests used to arrive on Sundays. For their first night's dinner, they were treated to Bud's "bare-chested" barbeques. It was the 1940's and the lodge deck had not been built yet. Bud and Roblay set up a grill over the outdoor stone fireplace near the pond on the side closest to the road. There was a hand-held rectangular metal grate, which Bud held over the fire while he cooked T-bone steaks, all the while talking with guests. And he was often shirtless since he got so warm near the fire. Bud was a robust man with a tanned, chiseled physique, and he and Roblay made an attractive couple. Bud usually didn't mingle with the guests much during the rest of the week, leaving Roblay to charm them as hostess, but he reigned over the barbeque. Chairs and picnic tables with red gingham cloths were set up on the other side of the pond. The staff would bring a cart down from the kitchen with polenta, sliced tomatoes and biscuits or garlic bread to accompany the steaks on a buffet. The street alongside Lake Creek Lodge was a dirt road at the time, so if it was dry and hot, a car would go by and dust would blow over from the street. Guests would cover their dinners with napkins until the dust subsided. Needless to say, pavement was a welcome modern amenity for mealtimes.

And so began the long tradition of Lake Creek Lodge's nightly summer dinners, originally for guests only, included as part of their accommodations. Eventually the first night's dinner was moved to the lodge when the new deck was built, and arrival day moved to Saturday. Mothers loved the fact that they didn't have to cook dinner for a week. During the day, adults and kids would try to peek at the chalkboard in the kitchen to see that night's dinner menu. Kids lined up to pull the rope for the dinner bell which clanged at 7 p.m., signaling to guests who were gathered on porches that dinner was ready. Screen doors slammed, kids ran across the lawn, and since Lake Creek did not originally have a liquor license, adults grabbed the bottles of wine they had brought with them from home for dinner. Dinner was served buffet-style, with the kids' table lining up first. Desserts were served plated to each table.

Oven-Fried Chicken replaced steaks as the first dinner. There was no printed recipe for Blanche's fried chicken, but fortunately Diana had committed it to memory. In the morning, Blanche would dredge chicken parts in flour seasoned with salt, pepper and paprika. Then she'd fry it in batches and put it in the cooler. Before dinner, she'd finish cooking the chicken in the oven. Blanche always

Blanche in the Lake Creek Lodge kitchen

KITCHEN STAFF

Blanche Williams:

Hired to cook four days a week. She left for a while, then returned full-time in the early 1970's and increased to six days a week. Blanche was responsible for most of the recipes in this book, and it was her long reign as cook that left its indelible mark on Lake Creek Lodge.

Clarence Walker:

Known by everyone as Walker, he was hired in the 1990's and cooked three days a week for about five years. Walker realized his love of baking in the Lake Creek kitchens.

included some livers and giblets on the platter with the chicken, and hers were so good that even kids who didn't eat them the rest of the year would give them a try.

The Ice Cream Cake with "Lake Creek" Chocolate Sauce could have an entire chapter devoted to it. That dessert *is* Lake Creek Lodge. It's a simple chocolate sheet cake, layered with vanilla ice cream and drizzled with a bitter dark chocolate sauce. But every bite is incredible and transports us all back over years and years of lodge dinners. (The chocolate sauce usually made another appearance later in the week for Friday night's Ice Cream Sundaes). The dessert disappeared from the menu during changes in the kitchen. That was one of our saddest losses, so including the Ice Cream Cake recipe became a high priority.

BAKING POWDER BISCUITS

Makes 15 biscuits

These biscuits were served every Sunday night with the Oven-Fried Chicken. The dough rolls out easily. Blanche always cut her biscuits with a juice glass, but a round 2 1/2-inch cookie cutter works just as well. There were six recipe cards for these biscuits, all with identically brief instructions, so they were obviously a staple over the years.

2 cups flour
4 teaspoons baking powder
1/2 teaspoon salt
1/2 cup shortening or cold unsalted butter, cut into bits
milk as needed (about 1/2 cup)

Preheat oven to 350°F.

Mix and sift flour, baking powder, and salt. Cut in shortening until thoroughly blended. Add milk gradually and mix to a soft dough with a fork. Roll out on a lightly floured board to 1/2-inch thickness. Cut with a biscuit cutter (or juice glass), and place on an ungreased baking sheet.

Bake 12–14 minutes, until golden brown.

LAKE CREEK LODGE SALAD

Makes enough dressing for a very large group with plenty leftover.

Also referred to as "Roblay's Salad," this was one of her specialties. According to Diana, Roblay insisted the lettuce leaves be broken into pieces, not cut with a knife. And when she tossed the salad, the kitchen help had to watch and learn the proper technique. They remember Roblay standing on the counter to pour the oil into the big mixer because she was too short to easily manage it from the floor.

Mayonnaise:

   1 raw egg, room temperature

   ¼ cup red wine vinegar

   2 tablespoons dry mustard

   2 tablespoons paprika

   2 tablespoons Beau Monde seasoning

   1 tablespoon salt

   1 tablespoon freshly ground black pepper

   1 tablespoon onion powder

   5–6 cups vegetable oil

French Dressing:

   ⅓ cup red wine vinegar

   ⅔ cup vegetable oil

   salt and freshly ground black pepper

   Worcestershire sauce to taste

Salad:

> Variety of lettuce, such as romaine, butter, garden chicory
> (Roblay figured 1 head of lettuce for every 5 people)
> 1 hardboiled egg to each head off lettuce,
> grated on fine grater

Prepare the Mayonnaise: Place the raw egg, vinegar and seasonings in a small mixing bowl. Beat at high speed until well blended. Start adding oil, still at high speed, slowly at first, then faster as mayonnaise starts to thicken. When the mixing bowl is full, you should have the proper proportions. Taste and correct.

Prepare the French Dressing: Whisk the red wine vinegar, oil and seasoning in a small bowl. Set aside.

Prepare the Salad: Wash lettuce, and separate leaf from leaf. Do not let it get too wet. Break leaves lightly and gently into smallish pieces (do not slice with a knife). Shake fairly dry in cloth. Place in dry cloth and refrigerate until dry and crisp. Lettuce should be completely dry to make a good salad.

Place lettuce in a large bowl with lots of room to toss lightly from the bottom. Put grated egg on top and season lavishly with salt, freshly ground black pepper, Beau Monde and onion powder. Mix lightly, then add enough French dressing to coat the leaves nicely, then add some mayonnaise on top. Toss very lightly and thoroughly, taste for seasoning, and serve at once.

The recipe takes patience, as the oil needs to be added very slowly while beating the mayonnaise for the dressing; resist the temptation to just pour it all in at once.

OVEN-FRIED CHICKEN

Serves 6–8

This recipe requires some advance planning, but it's well worth it for tender fried chicken. Blanche's method of frying the chicken in the morning, and then finishing it off in the oven just before dinner was a clever way to spread out her work since the time-consuming salad and cake that accompanied this meal needed to be assembled as well. And the kitchen was undoubtedly much cooler on a crisp mountain morning, making the task of frying more bearable than in the late afternoon. Blanche most likely used lard to fry the chicken, but a neutral oil works just as well. The smells wafting from the kitchen fans kept us day-dreaming of that night's dinner.

2 (3-pound) chickens, each cut into 8 pieces

1 quart buttermilk

2 cups all-purpose flour

1 tablespoon salt

2 teaspoons freshly ground black pepper

1 teaspoon paprika

oil for frying (such as peanut oil)

Start ahead by covering the chicken in buttermilk and refrigerating overnight.

Place the chicken pieces in a large bowl and pour the buttermilk over them so they are submerged. Cover with plastic wrap and refrigerate overnight.

Preheat the oven to 350°F.

In a large bowl, combine the flour, salt, pepper and paprika. Lift the chicken from the buttermilk, shaking off excess buttermilk, and roll each piece around in the flour mixture to coat completely.

Heat 1-inch of oil in a large stockpot over medium-high heat until it reaches a temperature of 350°F (you can use a candy thermometer to test the temperature).

Working in small batches, carefully fry the chicken a few pieces at a time for about 3 minutes on each side or until light brown. Adjust the heat in order to keep the oil at the same temperature since it will cool off when the cold chicken is added. Remove chicken from the oil and place on a rack set on a sheet pan. Continue with the remaining chicken pieces, making sure the oil is hot before each batch. (At this point, you can refrigerate the chicken for baking later if desired).

Bake chicken for 30–40 minutes (45–50 minutes if it has been in the refrigerator for several hours), until chicken is fully cooked. Serve immediately.

MASHED POTATOES

Serves 4–6

Mashed potatoes and gravy were often served on two nights to accompany the Oven-Fried Chicken and the Roast Turkey.

> 3 pounds Yukon Gold or Russet potatoes,
>   peeled and cut in half
> 1 cup milk or half-and-half
> 6 tablespoons unsalted butter
> salt and freshly ground black pepper

Place the potatoes in a large pot and cover with cold water and a teaspoon of salt. Bring to a boil, and cook until potatoes are tender when pierced with sharp knife, about 15–20 minutes.

Drain well in a colander. Meanwhile, add the milk and butter to the pan over medium heat, and sprinkle with salt and pepper. When the butter is melted, remove the pan from the heat. Run the potatoes through a ricer or food mill over the pan, or add them directly to the pan and use a masher. Use a wooden spoon to stir the potatoes into the butter and milk. Taste for seasoning and serve warm.

To hold for later, place potatoes in a heatproof bowl set over a pan of water over low heat. Cover the potatoes tightly with foil.

GRAVY

Makes 2 cups

This is a simple gravy that was served over white rice alongside Roast Pork Loin, or over Mashed Potatoes with the Roast Turkey or Oven-Fried Chicken.

reserved roasting pan with pan juices

3 tablespoons butter

3 tablespoons flour

2 cups chicken stock

¼ cup red or white wine

salt and freshly ground black pepper

If using a sheet pan for Oven-Fried Chicken, pour pan juices into a saucepan.

Skim the fat from the pan juices and discard. With the roasting pan positioned over two burners on medium heat, add ½ cup water. Boil for 2 minutes, scraping the bottom of the pan with a wooden spoon or spatula. Strain into a bowl and reserve.

In a medium saucepan, melt the butter until foamy, add the flour and whisk for 1 minute. Add the reserved pan juices and the stock, and whisk for 3–5 minutes. Add the wine and continue whisking until smooth and thickened. Taste for seasoning, adding salt and pepper if needed.

PEAS WITH SHALLOTS

Serves 8

The vegetable side dishes served in the early days reflected the times; they were simple and often over-cooked. Frozen peas were common, and while they worked just fine alongside the entrees, these are altered slightly for added flavor.

1 tablespoon olive oil
1 tablespoon unsalted butter
3 medium shallots, thinly sliced
1 (16-ounce) package frozen peas
⅓ cup water
salt and freshly ground black pepper

Heat oil and butter in a large skillet over medium heat, add shallots and sauté until soft, about 5 minutes. Stir in the peas and water and cook, covered, stirring occasionally until peas are tender, 3–5 minutes. Season with salt and pepper to taste.

ICE CREAM CAKE

Makes 2 cakes; Serves 20

This was one of the most popular Lake Creek Lodge desserts, fondly remembered by longtime guests. It's a simple chocolate sheet cake, layered with vanilla ice cream, then sliced thinly and drizzled with a dark chocolate sauce. In the old days, ice cream was delivered in bricks; the original cake took its dimensions based on those bricks.

> ¾ cup cocoa
> ¾ cup boiling water
> ½ cup shortening or butter, room temperature
> 2 cups sugar
> 2 eggs
> 1 ½ teaspoons baking soda
> 1 cup buttermilk
> 1 ¾ cup flour
> 1 teaspoon vanilla
> 1 ¼ teaspoon salt
> 1.5 quart vanilla ice cream (1 container)
> "Lake Creek" Chocolate Sauce (page 26)

Preheat oven to 350°F. Grease and flour a 12 x 17-inch sheet pan with sides.

Mix together the cocoa and boiling water, then set aside to cool.

Cream the butter and sugar, then add the eggs until incorporated.

In a separate bowl, stir the baking soda into the buttermilk. Add the buttermilk mixture to the egg mixture, alternating with the flour.

Add the reserved cocoa mixture until blended, then add the vanilla and salt.

Pour batter into the prepared sheet pan and bake until a toothpick comes out clean, 18–20 minutes. Place sheet pan on a rack to cool. (Cake can be wrapped in plastic wrap once cooled, and kept for a day before assembling with ice cream).

Cut the cake into three rectangles lengthwise, each one measuring 4 x 16-inches, then cut each rectangle in half vertically to yield six pieces measuring 4 x 8-inches. Soften the ice cream so that it is easier to spread.

Have two 9 x 5-inch loaf pans on hand for assembly

To assemble the cakes:

Lay one piece of cake inside a loaf pan measuring 9 x 5-inches. Spread a thick layer of ice cream over it, approximately ½–¾ inch deep. Cover with a piece of cake, and layer more ice cream on top as before. Then cap with a third piece of cake. The cake should be even with, or slightly above, the level of the pan. Cover with plastic wrap and freeze until hardened. Repeat with the remaining three pieces of cake and ice cream in the other loaf pan.

When frozen, invert the cakes onto a large cutting board. With a sharp knife, cut the ice cream cakes vertically into 1-inch slices, and lay each slice on a plate. Spoon warm chocolate sauce over the top before serving.

"LAKE CREEK" CHOCOLATE SAUCE

Makes about 1 cup

This recipe is similar to one in the original Joy of Cooking *cookbook, but most of us never knew that. We referred to it as "Lake Creek chocolate sauce" and we thought it was so special once a year. It's a distinctive dark chocolate sauce and was always used on the Ice Cream Cake and then later on ice cream sundaes.*

    4 ounces Baker's unsweetened chocolate

    1 cup brown sugar

    ½ cup heavy cream

The sauce is memorable for its bittersweet, slightly grainy texture.

Melt the chocolate over low heat, then stir in the sugar and cream. Cook until the sauce is thick, stirring constantly with a whisk.

Cool and refrigerate. Reheat for serving.

DAY 2

SUNDAY MENU

Management, Cabins & "The Girls"

Easy French Bread
French Onion Soup
Grilled New York Steaks
Creamy Polenta
Sliced Tomatoes & Cucumbers
Velvety Chocolate Pudding

A S AN OWNER, ROBLAY MCMULLEN RAN A TIGHT SHIP but we all benefited from her high standards and great taste. After she and Bud inherited the resort in 1937 and turned it into a little jewel, they ran it with style and grace. In 1955 Bud passed away, after working alongside Roblay for many years. Roblay, a petite woman with a larger-than-life personality, continued operating Lake Creek Lodge until she sold the property in 1974.

Roblay was brutally honest, but her devoted staff appreciated her work ethic. Ask any guest, and they would agree that if Roblay liked you, there wasn't anything she wouldn't do for you. But if she didn't like you, you weren't welcome at Lake Creek Lodge. She was known for her quick wit, feisty moods and sometimes sharp tongue. If you were the lucky recipient of her letters in later years, elegantly penned at her desk overlooking the swift-moving creek, they were full of advice and observations on the changing seasons outside her window.

Roblay always greeted us upon arrival and made sure our cabins were in order, using the "white-glove" treatment for checking the thoroughness of her staff. Roblay oversaw the creation of large natural arrangements in the lodge — in the entry, on the mantle over the stone fireplace and on the main magazine table. She and her staff would gather vine maple branches, pine cones and greenery from the property to create stunningly beautiful, rustic arrangements. Roblay was opinionated and set the bar high for her help, the food and the accommodations, and she had equally high expectations for her guests.

But the knotty-pine cabins were not without their idiosyncrasies, which we all grew to love. For some reason the bathrooms seemed the most memorable. The tiny sinks had separate spouts for (scalding) hot and (ice) cold water, so washing your face with warm water meant creating a cup with your hand and quickly racing it back and forth under the running water. The showers often had huge daddy-long-legs lurking in them, much to the chagrin of the kids who didn't want to be in the shower in the first place ("Why doesn't swimming in the pond count as a shower?!").

The wooden screen doors had a unique sound when they banged shut, that to this day still reminds guests of summertime. Screens also enclosed the much-loved sleeping porches, which were outfitted with cots, simple wooden dressers and tables. Many guests preferred these bedrooms to fall asleep with the gentle, gurgling sound of the creek and the heavy, wool Lake Creek blankets as a barrier against the chilly night air.

Sometimes kids would take sleeping bags out onto the canvas chaise lounges near the pond. The chaises were metal and difficult to move, with natural canvas stretched tight with rope. The canvas would squeak a little as you settled in, but they always dried in the sun if guests had wet suits. And they made great cots for a sleep-out under the stars. Of course, at night the bats swooped overhead, barely visible in the dark after dinner. But the lights in the trees would catch glimpses of them flying over the pond.

Keeping Lake Creek running smoothly was a well-trained staff under the very watchful eye of Roblay and her eventual manager, Glenna. "The Girls" as they were called, were usually college girls who came to live in the quarters behind the lodge and work at Lake Creek during their summer break. There was also a young man who was hired to help Bud and he was referred to by the staff as "The Boy."

One of The Girls was Bobsy Burns, the daughter of Bob and Patsy Burns, who grew up in Portland and spent summer vacations at Lake Creek. Bobsy recalls being paid $125 a month, minus $25 for boarding, to equal $100 a month plus tips. In those days, the tips for The Girls were an important part of their salary, left behind by grateful families.

Since Lake Creek was originally only a summertime resort, it was opened and closed for the season each year. The staff went through a grueling ritual, overseen by Roblay and Bud, to make sure that everything was in perfect shape both in the beginning and end of the season. They'd start at the top and work down: washing walls with bleach and water, and scrubbing every inch of the cabins.

And the rustic cabins were polished until they gleamed. Before and after each guest, The Girls would mop the hardwood floors and wash every window pane inside and out. They would clean and scrub the refrigerator, oven and stove, and wash and dry every dish and utensil. Then they'd make the beds, pulling the linens tightly into square corners just as Roblay had instructed them. The ashtrays would be cleaned and a fresh pack of matches would be placed inside each one. As thorough as this was, according to Bobsy, The Girls could get a cabin clean in 30 minutes if they wanted to.

The daily schedule was straightforward:

7:00 a.m.	Staff breakfast
7:30 a.m.	Clean the lodge
	Sweep the rocks, rake the gravel driveway and paths
	Clean bird droppings off the furniture
	Fill the hummingbird feeders on the dining deck
	Clean empty cabins
	Begin collecting leaves and branches for lodge arrangements (this took a lot of time since they'd take the truck and drive around looking for vine maple branches).
	Wash lodge windows (they used ammonia and water, and every pane probably got washed about 10 times over the course of the summer).
2:00 p.m.	Time off
6:00 p.m.	Work dinner until 9:00 p.m.

Often The Girls were hired by families to babysit children during afternoons to give parents a break.

Sunday night's dinner was a highlight. By now we were happily settled into our cabins and we'd had our first full day at Lake Creek Lodge. Soup was usually served more often in June and the end of August when it was a bit cooler. We could not locate a written recipe for the French Onion soup. Diana remembers it being canned beef broth and sautéed onions. Sometimes Walker added beef seasoning or more often he would save the juices from the previous week's Roast Prime Rib to add for flavor.

In July when it was hotter, the kitchen served more salads. On Sundays we'd often be served "junque" first: plates with carrot sticks, celery sticks and olives. This was followed by soup and homemade French bread. Blanche prepared several different pies and rotated them among the days. Desserts were the only variables each year

— they could switch days without causing a big stir among guests. Walker really enjoyed baking, and many of the dessert recipes were his. One day Diana asked Walker where he learned to bake and his reply was, "Here!"

Glenna on the lodge deck

MANAGEMENT STAFF

Kiyo:

Japanese by birth, Kiyo started working with Roblay in 1941 and stayed with her after Bud died to run the resort and cook.

Glenna Grace Peavy:

Hired in the mid-1960's as the manager, and cooked very capably on Blanche's day off.

Diana Pepperling:

Worked from 1974 to 2003, originally cleaning cabins and eventually as an assistant to Glenna until becoming manager in 1985. Diana retired in Sisters and has an incredible memory of details related to day-to-day operations.

EASY FRENCH BREAD

Makes 2 loaves

This bread does not need to rise, so it can be assembled and baked in less than an hour. It has a crunchy crust and soft interior, and was served sliced in baskets on the tables.

>   5 cups flour, divided in half
>   1 teaspoon sugar
>   1 tablespoon salt
>   3 tablespoons yeast
>   2 ½ cups very warm water (120°–130°F)
>   cornmeal for sprinkling on baking sheet
>   egg white for brushing (optional)

Preheat the oven to 450°F.

Combine 2 ½ cups of the flour, the sugar, salt and yeast in a mixer. Add the water and mix for 2–3 minutes on low speed until smooth.

Transfer to large bowl and add remaining 2 ½ cups flour. Knead and shape into 2 long loaves. Place loaves on baking sheet sprinkled liberally with cornmeal (the cornmeal keeps the bread from sticking, so use enough to coat the sheet). Brush with egg white if desired.

Bake for 20–25 minutes. Transfer to a rack to cool.

FRENCH ONION SOUP

Serves 6

This was a simple soup, ladled into bowls on the buffet line. Usually there was a bowl of grated cheese to sprinkle over the warm soup. Diana remembers the kitchen using canned beef broth, but sometimes Walker would save the juices from the previous week's Roast Prime Rib and add it to the soup for depth of flavor.

4 tablespoons butter

2 onions, thinly sliced

2 teaspoons flour

½ cup dry white wine

4 cups beef broth

1 ½ cups water

1 teaspoon Worcestershire sauce

salt and freshly ground black pepper

6 slices French bread (cut ½-inch thick)

1 cup shredded Gruyère cheese, plus
　　additional to sprinkle on top

Have additional grated cheese in a bowl to sprinkle on the soup.

Melt butter in a large saucepan over medium heat. Add the onions and sauté, stirring often, for 40–45 minutes, until tender and deep golden brown. Stir in the flour and cook for 1 minute. Add the wine and cook for another 2 minutes, scraping the dark bits off the bottom of the pan. Add the beef broth, water, Worcestershire sauce, salt and pepper to taste, and simmer for another 15–20 minutes.

Preheat oven to 350°F. Arrange bread slices on a baking sheet, and toast for 15 minutes, turning once, until bread is dry. Turn on broiler and sprinkle grated cheese on bread slices. Broil until cheese melts and turns light brown, about 2 minutes.

Ladle soup into bowls and top with bread slices.

GRILLED NEW YORK STEAKS

In the very early years, Bud presided over the outdoor barbequing of the steaks. They were grilled directly over high heat, which sealed in the juices and cooked the steaks quickly so they didn't dry out. Standing over the hot grills in the summertime July heat prompted a sweaty, muscular Bud to strip off his shirt, thus the nickname "Bare-Chested Barbecues" on steak night!

New York strip steaks, 1-inch thick
salt & freshly ground black pepper

These steaks embody the simplicity of lodge cooking — the setting was part of their appeal.

About an hour before grilling the steaks, take them out of the refrigerator and season with salt and pepper. Let them come to room temperature.

Prepare a barbeque for high heat. Transfer steaks with tongs to lightly oiled grill rack, and grill to desired doneness, uncovered, 5–6 minutes per side for medium rare (for a total cooking time of 10–12 minutes). Let steaks stand for 10 minutes before serving.

Bud presiding over the grill

CREAMY POLENTA

Serves 6

One of the signature recipes of the lodge, the very specific directions are exactly as Roblay dictated them years ago, and produce a flavorful, soft polenta. She used bacon drippings or butter for added flavor, so either is fine. The polenta is wonderful served alongside the Grilled New York Steaks, with freshly sliced tomatoes and cucumbers on the side.

3 cups milk

1 teaspoon salt

½ cup yellow cornmeal

1 tablespoon bacon drippings or unsalted butter

2–3 drops Tabasco sauce, to taste

½ teaspoon garlic salt

1 ¼ cups grated sharp cheddar cheese

This recipe doubles well and can be made ahead.

Preheat oven to 350°F. Grease an 8-inch square pan.

Heat milk in a saucepan over medium heat until it just starts to boil. Whisk in the salt and cornmeal. Add the drippings, Tabasco and garlic salt, and continue whisking until polenta is very thick like oatmeal and begins to pull away from the sides of the pan, about 10 minutes (it "pops" a lot during this process).

Pour into the prepared pan. Let cool for 2 minutes, then cover with the grated cheese. (If cheese goes on top right away, it melts right into the polenta. If it's too cool, it just sits on top. So semi-hot is just right).

Place in oven and bake for 30 minutes. Serve warm.

VELVETY CHOCOLATE PUDDING

Makes 9 servings

Walker also used this recipe as a filling for chocolate cream pie. Diana asked him what made his pudding so good, and he told her it was a secret. One day she walked into the kitchen just as Walker was pouring a package of marshmallows into a big batch of hot pudding. He made her swear up and down to secrecy and Diana never did tell anyone until she divulged the secret for this book. The marshmallows are added here as an optional ingredient, but they do make the pudding creamier.

> 1 cup sugar
>
> ¼ cup cornstarch
>
> ½ teaspoon salt
>
> 3 cups low fat milk
>
> 4 (1-ounce) squares semisweet chocolate, melted
>
> 4 large eggs
>
> 2 teaspoons butter
>
> 1 tablespoon vanilla extract
>
> ½ (16-ounce) package marshmallows (optional)

In a large, heavy saucepan, combine the sugar, cornstarch and salt. Whisk in the milk. Cook over moderately high heat, whisking occasionally, for about 5 minutes or until the mixture boils and thickens. Blend in the chocolate and set aside.

In a medium bowl, beat the eggs with an electric mixer on high until thick. Beat about 1 cup of the hot chocolate mixture into the eggs, then return the entire mixture to the saucepan. Cook, whisking, for about 3 minutes or until thick and smooth (do not boil). Remove from the heat and stir in the butter and vanilla, and marshmallows if using.

Serve warm or chilled.

DAY 3

MONDAY MENU

The Barn, Al the Wrangler & Horses

Zucchini Bread or Roblay's Orange Bread
Spinach Salad with Mustard Dressing
Roast Pork Loin
Homemade Chunky Applesauce
Rice with Gravy
Glazed Carrots
Fresh Fruit with Cookies

Hay Rides

Orange Crush
Toasted Marshmallows with Graham Crackers
"Sodey Pop"

HORSES USED TO BE A BIG PART OF THE LAKE CREEK experience, and many guests can still remember the names of their favorite (and not-so-favorite), horses. There was a big barn situated beyond the field above the lodge. And looking like he stepped right out of central casting was Al Hein, the wrangler who oversaw the barn and horses. He had leathery skin and was a legitimate cowboy. The kids both adored him and were mildly terrified of him.

Al's job included organizing horseback rides for the guests, the weeknight hay rides for the children and, perhaps most memorably for some, sitting at the kids' table during dinner. For the ten years that Al was wrangler, he dispensed trail lore at the head of the kids' table to an audience of children who were in awe of him and frightened of him at the same time. (Though not frightened enough to stop them from carrying out dinnertime shenanigans).

Al kept a little notebook in his pocket so kids could request which horse they wanted to ride the next day. Everyone had a favorite, and most of their names were memorable: Paint, Pepper, Buck, Sandy, Midnight, Skeeter, Snowball, Smokey, Silver, Roaney and Monty (who wore Bud's silver bridle). If kids were good and nice to Al, he would reward them by letting them groom the horses during the day. After dinner, Al would walk around the tables asking parents if their families wanted to ride the next day.

In the mornings, kids would meet up at the barn for the 9:15 a.m. rides. Sometimes the trail rides were led by Al, but often fathers would take kids out on their own. There were loads of different trails, some crossing the Metolius once

or twice. Kids went for rides three or four times a week, either on the 1-hour trail or (even better), the 2-hour trail. More than one guest remembers taking off on unplanned gallops and jumping logs while holding on for dear life. The day's rides always made for great stories at dinnertime, and they still provide some of the best memories today.

A young rider with Al

Once or twice a week, Al and The Girls took the kids on a hay ride. Just after dinner, he'd pull up in front of the lodge deck with a horse-drawn wagon filled with fresh hay. The kids would pile in, wave goodbye to their parents, and Al would lead the horses out along the Metolius River. The kids would toss hay around — much of it ending up in their pants and shirts which made for an itchy evening. By the time it was dark, they'd arrive at the campground fire pit, where one of The Girls had already built a fire. The menu never changed: Toasted marshmallows with graham crackers (you could bring your own chocolate), and "Sodey Pop" as Al called it. Originally it was non-carbonated Orange Ne-Hi or Grape Ne-Hi, and later it was Orange Crush.

Sadly, neither Al nor the horses remained at Lake Creek Lodge forever. In the late 1970's, the running of the barn was contracted out to Gil Ticolot who brought in his own horses. Eventually that ended and the barn was moved across the road. It is believed to be in the far corner of the Meadows, just past the old Reynolds home. A house was built in the barn's place, which they called The Stables.

Dessert at Lake Creek depended upon what fruit was in season, such as berries or slices of melon, or simply perfectly fresh, sweet peaches served with thick cream.

ZUCCHINI BREAD

Makes 2 loaves

 3 eggs, beaten
 1 cup vegetable oil
 2 cups sugar
 2 teaspoons vanilla
 2 cups grated zucchini (about 2 zucchini)
 ¾ cup chopped nuts
 3 cups flour
 1 teaspoon baking soda
 ½ teaspoon baking powder
 ½ teaspoon salt
 3 teaspoons ground cinnamon

Preheat oven to 350°F. Grease 2 loaf pans.

In a large bowl, beat together the eggs, oil and sugar. Stir in the vanilla, zucchini and nuts.

In a separate bowl, sift the flour, baking soda, baking powder, salt and cinnamon. Add to the wet ingredients and mix until just combined. Pour into prepared loaf pans.

Bake for 1 hour. Remove to a rack to cool in pans, then remove bread from pans to cool completely.

ROBLAY'S ORANGE BREAD

Makes 1 loaf

This bread has a hint of orange flavor and was served as an alternative to Zucchini Bread.

> 1 orange, rind grated
> 1 cup chopped pitted dates
> ½ cup chopped nuts
> ¾ cup sugar
> 2 tablespoons melted butter
> 1 egg
> 1 teaspoon vanilla
> 2 cups flour
> 1 teaspoon baking powder
> ½ teaspoon baking soda
> ½ teaspoon salt

Preheat oven to 350°F. Grease a loaf pan.

Extract the juice from the orange into a liquid measuring cup, then add enough boiling water to make 1 cup. Pour into a large bowl, then stir in the rind, dates and nuts. Set aside.

In a small bowl, blend the sugar, melted butter, egg, and vanilla, then add to the orange mixture.

Sift together the flour, baking powder, baking soda, and salt. Fold the dry ingredients into the orange mixture.

Pour batter into prepared loaf pan and bake for 1 hour. Test with a toothpick; bake a little longer if necessary until toothpick inserted into center comes out clean. Remove to a rack to cool in pan, then remove bread from pan to cool completely.

SPINACH SALAD WITH MUSTARD DRESSING

Serves 6–8

According to notes on the original recipe card, the lodge kitchen multiplied the ingredients by seven in order to feed a full crowd on the deck. And they used to "chill the spinach leaves in a tightly sealed plastic bag to keep them crisp."

Dressing:

> juice of 1 lemon
>
> 1 tablespoon Dijon mustard
>
> 1 tablespoon grated parmesan cheese
>
> 1 teaspoon sugar
>
> 1 teaspoon Worcestershire sauce
>
> ½ teaspoon salt
>
> freshly ground black pepper
>
> 2 tablespoons vegetable oil (or olive oil)

Salad:

> 1 pound fresh baby spinach
>
> ¼ pound fresh mushrooms, sliced
>
> 1 hard boiled egg white, sieved or chopped
>
> ¼ cup sunflower seeds

In a small bowl, whisk together all of the dressing ingredients.

In a large bowl, combine the spinach and mushrooms. Add the dressing and toss. Garnish with the chopped egg and sunflower seeds.

ROAST PORK LOIN

Serves 8

    1 (3-pound) boneless pork loin
    1 tablespoon finely chopped fresh rosemary
    2 teaspoons minced garlic
    salt and freshly ground black pepper
    1 ½ cups chicken stock

Preheat the oven to 375°F.

Mix together the rosemary, garlic and a generous amount of salt and pepper. Rub it all over the pork. Place pork on a rack in a roasting pan, and roast for 45 minutes.

Pour the stock into the pan and continue roasting, basting occasionally and adding more stock if necessary. Roast until an instant-read thermometer inserted into the center of the pork registers 155°F, about 45 more minutes.

Transfer the meat to a platter to rest for a few minutes before carving.

With the roasting pan positioned over two burners on medium heat, simmer until liquid reduces down a bit, scraping the bottom of the pan with a wooden spoon or spatula. Strain if necessary, and serve warm with the pork.

HOMEMADE CHUNKY APPLESAUCE

Makes 2 ½ cups

Washington is the largest apple-producing state, with nearby Oregon being an important producer and experimenter with new orchards. For applesauce, choose apples that have a tart-sweet flavor and flesh which falls apart easily when cooked. Varieties such as Gravenstein, Empire, McIntosh, Jonathan and Granny Smith make thick, flavorful sauces.

> 5 apples, peeled, cored and cut into eighths
> water
> 2 tablespoons freshly squeezed lemon juice
> 1 tablespoon plus 2 teaspoons granulated sugar

While cutting the apples, drop them into a quart of water with 1 tablespoon of the lemon juice to prevent browning.

Drain the apples and place them in a medium saucepan with 1 tablespoon of sugar and ⅓ cup water. Bring water to a boil, cover pan, reduce the heat and simmer, stirring occasionally, until apples are tender, about 15 minutes. Uncover the pan and simmer for another 8–10 minutes, until apples are soft enough to mash with a fork.

Drain off excess liquid. Mash apples with a fork against the side of the pan to chunky consistency. Add 1 tablespoon lemon juice and 2 teaspoons sugar. Taste and adjust for sweetness and flavor.

GLAZED CARROTS

Serves 6–8

If you can find thin baby carrots, just trim those and use them whole. Otherwise, cut large carrots on the diagonal into 1/2-inch slices. Cooking time may vary depending on the thickness of the carrots, but just know that if you happen to overcook the carrots you're staying true to tradition since that was the fate of many lodge vegetables!

2 tablespoons butter

2 tablespoons packed brown sugar

1 cup water

1 ½ lbs. carrots, peeled & sliced diagonally

salt and freshly ground black pepper

1 teaspoon fresh lemon juice

2 teaspoons fresh parsley, minced (optional)

In a medium skillet, bring the butter, sugar and water to a boil, stirring to dissolve sugar. Add the carrots and simmer, covered, until carrots are tender, about 5 minutes.

Using a slotted spoon, transfer carrots to a bowl and boil remaining liquid, uncovered, until reduced to about 2 tablespoons. Reduce heat to low, add carrots to glaze and toss to coat. Season with salt and pepper, and stir in the lemon juice. Sprinkle with the parsley if desired. Taste and adjust seasoning before serving hot or room temperature.

OATMEAL SCOTCHIES

Makes 4 dozen bars

Initially it was a surprise to see that this handwritten recipe was almost identical to the one printed on the back of today's bag of Nestlé butterscotch morsels. But then it made sense: Fifty years ago novelty convenience foods were being embraced by busy cooks both at home and in busy lodges. These chewy, golden bars with their caramel flavor are irresistible and immediately bring back sweet memories.

> 1 cup butter (2 sticks), softened to room temperature
> ¾ cup sugar
> ¾ cup packed light brown sugar
> 2 eggs
> 1 teaspoon vanilla
> 1 ¼ cups flour
> 1 teaspoon baking soda
> ½ teaspoon salt
> ½ teaspoon cinnamon
> 3 cups oats (uncooked)
> 1 (11-ounce) package butterscotch chips

Preheat oven to 375°F.

In a mixing bowl fitted with the paddle attachment, beat the butter and sugars until creamy, about 3 minutes. Add the eggs and vanilla and beat until incorporated.

In a small bowl, combine the flour, baking soda, salt and cinnamon. Beat into the butter mixture. Stir in the oats and butterscotch chips.

Grease a 15 x 10 x 1-inch sheet pan. Spread the dough into the pan. Bake for 18–22 minutes, or until light brown. Cool in pan on a rack, then cut into bars.

LEMON BARS

Makes one 9 x 9-inch pan

The kitchen's original recipe calls for coconut in the filling, which adds a surprisingly nice texture to the classic lemon bar. You can bake these ahead, chill them, and sprinkle with powdered sugar just before serving.

Crust:

>1 cup flour
>¼ cup powdered sugar
>½ cup (1 stick) cold sweet butter, cut into eight pieces

Filling:

>2 eggs, beaten
>1 cup sugar
>3 tablespoons freshly squeezed lemon juice (about 2 lemons)
>grated zest of 1 lemon
>3 tablespoons flour
>½ teaspoon baking powder
>1 ½ cups shredded coconut
>powdered sugar for dusting

Preheat the oven to 350°F.

Combine the flour and powdered sugar in the bowl of an electric mixer fitted with the paddle attachment. Add the butter and mix on low speed until mixture resembles coarse crumbs. Press crust into bottom of a 9 x 9-inch pan.

Bake crust for 20 minutes, or until golden brown.

In a large bowl, whisk together the eggs and sugar. Stir in the lemon juice, zest, flour, and baking powder until combined, then add the coconut and mix well. Pour the filling evenly over the top of the crust.

Return lemon bars to the oven and bake for 20 minutes, until the filling is set. Allow to cool, then slice into squares and sprinkle with powdered sugar.

To evenly dust powdered sugar over the top of the bars, use a small strainer and tap the sides gently.

CHOCOLATE CHIP COOKIES

Makes 5 dozen cookies

    1 ⅓ cups butter, softened to room temperature

    1 cup sugar

    1 cup light brown sugar, packed

    2 eggs

    2 teaspoons vanilla

    3 ½ cups flour

    1 teaspoon baking soda

    1 teaspoon salt

    1 (12-ounce) package chocolate chips

Preheat oven to 350°F.

In the bowl of a mixer fitted with the paddle attachment, cream butter and sugars together until light and fluffy, about 2 minutes. Beat in eggs and vanilla.

In another bowl, sift together the flour, baking soda and salt. Beat into the butter mixture until incorporated. Stir in the chocolate chips. Chill dough for at least 1 hour.

Scoop rounded teaspoons of dough and place on ungreased baking sheet. Bake 12–14 minutes. Let cookies cool on baking sheet for 5 minutes, then remove to rack to cool.

BLANCHE'S SNICKERDOODLES

Makes 4 dozen cookies

While this is the original recipe, Blanche often deviated from the instructions and mixed some cinnamon into the dough rather than rolling the balls in the coating. But this traditional version makes a light, buttery cookie and even a large batch will disappear quickly they are so good.

> 1 cup butter, softened to room temperature
>
> 1 ½ cups sugar
>
> 2 eggs
>
> 2 ¾ cups flour
>
> 2 teaspoons cream of tartar
>
> 1 teaspoon baking soda
>
> ¼ teaspoon salt

Coating:

> 2 tablespoons sugar
>
> 1 ½ teaspoons cinnamon

Preheat oven to 350°F.

In the bowl of an electric mixer fitted with the paddle attachment, cream the butter and sugar until light and fluffy. Add the eggs and mix until smooth. Stir together the flour, cream of tartar, baking soda and salt, and add to the batter.

In a small bowl, mix the sugar & cinnamon coating together.

Line a baking sheet with parchment paper. Shape dough into 1-inch balls and roll in sugar-cinnamon mix. Place balls a few inches apart on baking sheet — about one dozen on each sheet.

Bake 8–10 minutes.

BROWNIES

Makes 20 brownies

There were two different brownie recipes in the old recipe box. This one was the favorite during testing — a traditional, dense brownie that doesn't crumble and is great with a scoop of vanilla ice cream. Since this recipe called for oleo, another term for margarine, it was truly one of the old ones.

> 4 ounces Baker's unsweetened chocolate
> 1 ½ sticks butter
> ½ teaspoon salt
> 2 cups sugar
> 3 eggs
> 1 teaspoon vanilla
> 1 cup flour
> 1 cup chopped nuts (walnuts or pecans)

Preheat the oven to 350°F. Generously butter a 9 x 13-inch pan.

In a small pan over very low heat, melt the chocolate, butter and salt, whisking occasionally, just until the chocolate is melted. Remove from the heat to cool.

In a large bowl, whisk together the sugar, eggs and vanilla until smooth. Whisk in the melted chocolate mixture. Stir in the flour just until it disappears, then stir in the nuts.

Pour batter into the prepared pan and bake for 35 minutes, or until a toothpick inserted in the center comes out clean. Remove to a rack to cool completely before cutting into squares.

Hellyer fishing trip - Aug. '46

DAY 4

TUESDAY MENU

Fishing & Swimming in the Pond

Popovers
Fruit Plate with "Caribbean" Fruit Sauce
Prime Rib
Oven-Browned Potato Wedges
Green Beans
Carrot Cake with Cream Cheese Icing

SUMMER DAYS AT LAKE CREEK WERE, AND CONTINUE to be, a paradise for kids. We could scamper all over the place and, as long as we could swim if we fell into the pond, we were given a lot of independence.

The pond was the main gathering place for fishing and swimming since the pool was only built in recent years. The pond was man-made by diverting a segment of Lake Creek. The creek was split, with part going into the pond, and the other part spilling over a small wood dam which bypassed the pond. There was a narrow bridge across the creek at the fork, and it would sway and bounce as we ran across it. At the other side of the pond, under the larger bridge, another wooden dam would allow pond water to spill-off back into Lake Creek, where it would meet-up with the by-passed creek and continue down. In this way, the pond had a continual supply of fresh water from the creek, and the shallow end would stay especially clear from this movement.

The deeper part of the pond grew darker and was prone to filling with seaweed, so each summer Roblay and Bud would dredge the pond and pull out the growth. The dredging was a big deal. Bud would remove the dam by the bridge next to the water wheel so that almost all of the water was drained out of the pond. Then he'd hitch up two big horses to a plow. He'd drive the horses and plow into the mud of the pond and dredge out the mess to make it deep again. Despite the dredging, the deeper end was always dark, so parents would need to be careful with smaller

children. The shallow end had a small bridge spanning the creek so that kids could get to the pale blue slide that sat at the edge of the pond on its own little island.

Swimming in the pond was entertaining since there was also a large wooden raft in the middle of the deeper end. Older kids and parents would jump off the wooden deck and swim to the raft. Often after dinner, teenagers would jump in the pond and gather on the raft to play King of the Hill by trying to flip the raft. And we discovered (much to management's chagrin), that if we temporarily lifted the wooden dams on hot afternoons, we could create small rapids in the creek bypass and ride them on inner tubes. Tubing down Lake Creek continues to be entertainment for older kids, as it eventually meets up with the Metolius where we disembark around Camp Sherman with legs and hands numbed from the icy cold water.

Fishing was also a big part of life around the pond for kids. The pond was stocked each spring with rainbow trout. There was a wooden sign posted on the deck of the deeper end that said "Limit 3 fish per child." Kids would often get out of bed in the morning and head out in their pajamas with a fishing rod to try and catch something before breakfast. The lodge kitchen staff would clean the fish we caught, and then cook it as a personal treat for dinner that night.

The pond and creek were home to crawdads, and the boys especially enjoyed spending hours building crawdad traps and using nets to catch crawdads. They'd put them in buckets, and then release them a little while later. Adults fly-fished in nearby rivers.

The running creek could be heard in almost every cabin, day and night. That was, and still is, one of the most important aspects of Lake Creek Lodge. The pond was eventually removed, a new one created above the cabins for fishing, and the creek restored to its natural habitat. But the sound of the water remains. Pale blue forget-me-nots line the banks of the creek, another symbol of Lake Creek. And the wild spearmint along the edges was picked by the staff for cooking. Walks along the river are common, and the lodge staff has created new paths that go farther down the river and cross it, especially as new cabins have been built.

As for dinner, Walker would slice the prime rib for each guest outside on the lodge deck. He didn't have time to change his dirty apron, and would get so warm with the heat lamp over the meat that he'd start to sweat. We'd often wonder if the sweat dripped onto our meat.

Jeff Severeide and Lou Rems

GROUNDS STAFF

Art Scofield:

Hired around 1970 to work maintenance and care for the lawns.

Lou Rems:

Hired in 1978 for maintenance and knew everything about the place. Lou spent his days mowing the lawns, moving sprinklers, making cabin repairs, and building in the off-season.

Jeff Severeide:

Also part of the good-natured maintenance crew and willing to take on any task.

POPOVERS

Makes 12 popovers

These much-anticipated popovers would arrive on the tables on Prime Rib night. They were often devoured quickly, which left an empty basket by the time the entrée arrived. This in turn motivated some of the most ardent fans to employ "search and rescue" methods in hopes of securing extras from diners exercising more self-restraint.

    2 eggs
    1 cup milk
    1 cup flour
    ½ teaspoon salt

These are best when prepared just before eating.

Preheat oven to 425°F.

Grease a 12-cup muffin tin very well with butter, rubbing about a ½ teaspoon of butter in each cup. Place muffin tin in oven while making batter.

Beat eggs slightly, then add the milk, flour and salt. Beat just until smooth (do not overbeat). Remove muffin tin from oven and fill each cup about halfway. Immediately return to oven and bake 15 minutes until popped and golden. Reduce heat to 350°F and continue baking for 15–20 minutes, or until popovers are puffed and deep golden brown.

Remove from pan immediately and serve hot.

"CARIBBEAN" FRUIT SAUCE

Makes 2 cups

About once during the week, a platter of fresh fruit was set out on the buffet accompanied by a bowl of very thick, creamy sauce. We would ladle the mystery sauce over the fruit, knowing only that it was really good. It turns out a key ingredient was marshmallow creme, and for kids this no doubt upped the consumption of fruit. The recipe called for orange liqueur, which gave it a subtle sweetness. Perhaps that's why the kitchen referred to this as the "Caribbean" sauce — they likely used Curaçao, an orange-flavored liqueur from the Caribbean. Eventually Velda became concerned about using the liqueur with children, so the kitchen switched to orange juice concentrate. Some adults thought it was never as good as the original, but kids seem to prefer the orange juice version since it's reminiscent of an orange creamsicle.

    1 cup heavy whipping cream

    1 (7-ounce) container marshmallow creme

    2 tablespoons frozen orange juice
        concentrate, slightly thawed

    or 2 tablespoons orange liqueur

Whip the cream with a hand-held beater until stiff peaks form. Add the marshmallow creme and beat for one more minute on low speed until smooth. Stir in the orange juice concentrate or liqueur, taste and add more for stronger flavor if desired.

Serve immediately with fresh fruit, or cover and chill. Sauce can be chilled up to 1 day. Stir before serving if it separates a bit.

PRIME RIB

Serves 12–14

For many guests, our most vivid memory of Walker was when he presided over the prime rib carving in the buffet line. He was generous with his slices, and even young kids would walk away with a big slab of beef taking up most of their plate. For the best roast, ask the butcher for the loin end, preferably ribs 8 through 12.

> 1 (5-rib) roast (about 10-12 pounds),
>   trimmed of excess but not all fat
> 2 tablespoons oil
> salt and freshly ground black pepper
> ½ cup chopped carrots
> ½ cup chopped onions
> 2 cups beef stock

Remove the meat from the refrigerator 1–2 hours before cooking to bring it to room temperature.

Preheat the oven to 425°F. Place roast fat side up (bone side down) in a roasting pan just large enough to hold the beef. Rub the exposed ends of the roast with the oil and sprinkle all over with salt and pepper.

Place the roast in the oven for 15 minutes. Turn the heat down to 325°F, baste the ends of the meat with the fat from the pan, and cook for another 45 minutes. Scatter the carrots and onion around the beef and baste them with the pan juices. Roast for about 1 more hour. Begin checking meat in several places with an instant-read thermometer, roasting until the desired temperature: 125°F for rare, 130°F for medium-rare, and 140°F for medium. (The temperature of the meat will rise about 5 degrees in the time that it sits out of the oven before carving).

Remove the roast to a carving board, discard trussing strings, and let rest for 15 minutes, tented with foil.

To make the au jus sauce, skim most of the fat from the roasting pan. Place the pan on a burner over high heat. Pour in the beef stock and bring to a boil, scraping up the brown bits and mashing the vegetables into the liquid, about 5 minutes. Pour everything through a fine mesh strainer into a small saucepan, and simmer for several more minutes. Taste for seasoning and serve with the meat.

Walker had au jus in a bowl for guests to spoon over their meat. To make a sour cream-horseradish sauce to serve alongside the beef, stir a little bottled horseradish, Dijon mustard and salt into a bowl of sour cream.

OVEN-BROWNED POTATO WEDGES

Serves 6–8

Dividing the potato wedges among two rimmed baking sheets prevents overcrowding and allows the potatoes to form a crispy brown crust. You could toss the potatoes with minced fresh rosemary leaves before roasting for some added flavor.

  3 pounds unpeeled russet potatoes (about 8)
  3 tablespoons olive oil
  3 tablespoons butter, melted
  salt and freshly ground black pepper

Preheat oven to 400°F.

Slice each potato lengthwise into 8 wedges. Divide wedges between two large rimmed baking sheets, arranging them in a single layer. Drizzle equally with the olive oil and butter, and toss to coat. Sprinkle with a generous amount of salt and pepper and toss again.

Roast wedges in middle of oven until tender inside and browned in spots, turning occasionally, about 45 minutes. Sprinkle with more salt and pepper if needed, and serve hot.

GREEN BEANS

Serves 8

A simple recipe which lets the beans speak for themselves when they are at their prime in the summer. For a variation, add sliced onions or garlic to the sauté pan just before the beans.

1 ½ pounds green beans, stems trimmed
1 tablespoon olive oil
2 teaspoons butter
salt and freshly ground black pepper

Bring a large saucepan of salted water to a boil. Have a large bowl filled with ice water ready nearby.

Add the green beans to the boiling water and cook, uncovered, 5 minutes or until crisp-tender. Drain and immediately transfer the beans to the bowl of ice water to stop cooking, then drain well and roll between paper towels to dry.

Heat oil and butter in a 12-inch skillet over medium heat. Add the beans and sauté until just tender, 2–3 minutes. Season with salt and pepper to taste and serve immediately.

CARROT CAKE WITH
CREAM CHEESE ICING

Serves 10–12

The handwritten notes on the original recipe card read, "Pour into old enamel baking pan." The lodge kitchen had heavy pans and cast iron skillets that were used so often over the years that each served specific purposes known to the staff. The recipe also called for a #303 can of crushed pineapple, which is roughly equivalent to a 20-ounce can nowadays.

Cake:

    3 eggs

    1 ½ cups vegetable oil

    2 cups sugar

    2 teaspoons vanilla extract

    1 cup chopped nuts

    1 (20-ounce) can crushed pineapple, drained (about 2 cups)

    1 cup shredded coconut

    2 cups shredded carrots (about 3–4 carrots)

    2 cups flour

    2 teaspoons cinnamon

    2 teaspoons baking soda

    1 teaspoon salt

Icing:

    6 ounces cream cheese, softened to room temperature

    ½ cup butter (1 stick), softened to room temperature

    1 ½ pounds powdered sugar

    1 teaspoon vanilla

Preheat oven to 350°F. Grease and dust with flour a 9 x 13-inch (or slightly larger) baking pan.

In a large bowl, beat together the eggs, oil, sugar and vanilla. Stir in the nuts, pineapple, coconut and carrots and mix well.

In a separate bowl, sift together the flour, cinnamon, baking soda and salt. Add to the wet ingredients and stir well with a wooden spoon until well blended. Pour into prepared pan and bake for 1 hour.

Prepare the icing: Combine the cream cheese and butter in the bowl of a mixer. Add the powdered sugar and beat until fluffy. Beat in the vanilla. Ice the cake when cooled.

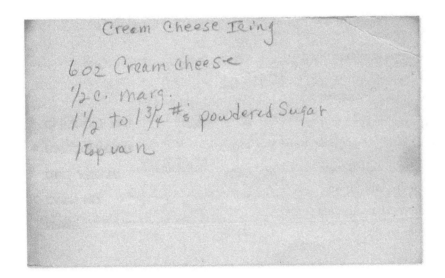

DAY 5

WEDNESDAY MENU

Kids at Lake Creek Lodge

Hard Cornbread
Green Salad with Tavern Vinaigrette
Roast Leg of Lamb
Lake Creek Mint Sauce
Curried Rice
White Rice with Gravy
Sautéed Carrots, Celery & Onions
Blueberry Buckle

KIDS END UP WITH A LOT OF MEMORIES FROM LAKE Creek Lodge, and it is often the small things that create the most lasting impressions.

Biking to Camp Sherman was an important part of each day. Lake Creek Lodge used to have a few old, rickety bikes out in front of the lodge for guests to borrow. We remembered them as being too big for kids, and we needed to peddle standing up if we couldn't reach the seat. Fortunately, the general store at Camp Sherman has stayed largely the same, selling just enough food, fishing supplies, and perhaps most importantly, candy and ice cream. Most kids biked down with a pocket full of change to carefully choose from the bins of penny candy. Candy necklaces were popular with the little girls. The freezer of ice cream bars remains popular with the kids and adults, especially when the treats are enjoyed on the brown wooden bench just outside the store next to the big, carved wooden bear.

Wednesday was also the day of the Weenie Roast. At noon, the staff would ring the bell and kids could go to the lodge deck for lunch where they were served grilled hot dogs, potato chips (both regular and BBQ), and Kool-Aid. Dessert was either Dixie cups filled with vanilla ice cream and orange sherbet along with a wooden spoon, or watermelon slices. If it was watermelon that day, lunch was followed by a watermelon seed-spitting contest. Sometimes after the kids were finished with lunch, their parents would use the grills to cook prime rib slices leftover from the night before for their own lunches.

During the week, some parents would arrange an adult picnic. This happened at various spots including Three Creeks Lake, or near the House on the Metolius. Food was gathered together — things like beef tenderloin sandwiches, cheese and crackers — and driven to a trail for a short walk into the picnic spot. The young children stayed behind and were looked after by  The Girls or other Lake Creek Lodge staff. The older kids were often left to their own devices, the parents probably figuring there wasn't much that could go wrong within the confines of the resort property.

And there were always lots of tennis games up at the courts involving teenagers and adults, often culminating in a tournament at the end of the week: Californians vs. Oregonians.

During lodge dinners, the kids were seated at their own long table. And sitting at the head of that table was Al the Wrangler. He'd wear a starched white shirt and pressed jeans with his cowboy boots. Al probably didn't want to sit at the kids' table, but Roblay made him sit there. He was wonderfully patient with the kids even when they poured sugar and salt in his drink, and crawled underneath the table.

The kids' table was near the end of the deck where we could hear the bug zapper at the back entrance to the kitchen. Once in a while a big bug would hit the zapper and really get fried. We also remember the Ritz crackers stacked in cracker trays and the balls of chilled butter. Once the kids' table was gone, kids sat with their parents and resorted to entertaining themselves by building houses out of the sugar packets on the table, and lathering their rolls with too much butter.

Sometimes the older kids found ways to have fun behind the backs of the adults. Sally Follen recalls a summer during World War II, when she and her friends used to sneak into the lodge kitchen at night. They'd turn on music and dance. One night when Sally hoisted herself onto the counter she hit her head on a cast iron skillet, which fell and broke. Bud was furious. Sally's mother looked all over Bend and Portland to try and replace the skillet, but they couldn't find one since iron was scarce during the war.

Wednesday's dinner had two very traditional recipes: Lake Creek Mint Sauce and Hard Cornbread. The mint sauce was made with the fresh mint growing along the creek. It was traditionally a sticky, slightly runny sauce, covering most of the plate, and it was the perfect accompaniment to the Roast Leg of Lamb. The Hard Cornbread is a bit trickier. Blanche could make it perfectly, but it's not always easy to replicate. The secret is to spread the batter thinly in the pan, bake it slowly, and break off crunchy outer pieces as they harden.

HARD CORNBREAD

Serves 8–10

Arguably the most unique of lodge recipes, these flat bread pieces have just a few ingredients. But the process takes time and a little practice to get the crispy but chewy texture. The trick is to spread the batter thinly and pay very close attention as it bakes to prevent overcooking. The result is well worth the effort. We remember digging way down into the basket for the "best" pieces — thinner and crispier for some, or thicker and chewier for others. This recipe doubles easily.

> 2 ½ cups cornmeal
> 1 stick salted butter, melted
> 1 teaspoon salt
> 5 cups boiling water

Preheat the oven to 350°F. Butter a large rimmed sheetpan.

Combine the cornmeal, butter and salt in a large bowl. Add the boiling water and mix. The consistency should be fairly runny — like thin icing. If it's too thick it won't spread easily in the pan, so add a little more water if necessary.

Using a spatula, pour and spread the batter thinly in the pan so that it is about ¼-inch thick.

Bake for approximately 20–30 minutes, checking periodically. Open the oven often to break off edges that are starting to brown and become crisp. The bread should break apart easily when done, yielding small- to medium-sized pieces. Keep baking the remainder, collecting pieces as they are ready.

Before serving, reheat the cornbread pieces in a warm oven just to heat them through, but not to soften.

So coveted was this bread that savvy kids would scout out tables with new guests (who would be unfamiliar with the "gold" wrapped in the basket on their table), and inquire if they did in fact want their cornbread. Untouched baskets were a windfall!

TAVERN VINAIGRETTE

Makes 1 cup

This is a red dressing, especially good on mixed greens or spinach salads.

¼ cup vinegar
¼ cup ketchup
1 teaspoon sugar
1 teaspoon Worcestershire sauce
2 teaspoons minced onion
1 clove garlic, minced
dash Tabasco sauce
½ cup vegetable oil

Combine all of the ingredients except the oil, either in a bowl with a whisk or in a blender, and whisk or process to combine. Add the oil in a steady stream, and whisk or process briefly until emulsified.

ROAST LEG OF LAMB

Serves 8–10

When it came to roasting meats, the Lake Creek Lodge kitchen let the meat speak for itself with simple seasoning and straightforward roasting. A highlight of the lamb dinner was the homemade Lake Creek Mint Sauce (page 71), which was always an accompaniment.

  1 (5–7 pound) leg of lamb (bone-in)
  6 cloves garlic, peeled and slivered
  salt and freshly ground black pepper

Preheat the oven to 400°F.

Trim as much of the fat from the lamb as possible. With the tip of a knife, make small ½-inch wide slits all over the meat, inserting a sliver of garlic into each hole. Season the lamb generously all over with salt and pepper, and place on a rack in a roasting pan.

Roast lamb for 30 minutes, then reduce the heat to 350°F. After an hour of roasting, begin checking the internal temperature by inserting an instant-read thermometer into the center of the meat without touching the bone. Continue checking every 10 minutes or so, until thermometer reaches 135°F–140°F for medium-rare (about 1 ½ hours total roasting time) or 145°F–150°F for medium.

Transfer meat to a serving platter and tent with foil for 15 minutes before carving (the temperature of the meat will rise while it rests. For well-done, let lamb rest 15 minutes longer).

LAKE CREEK MINT SAUCE

Makes 3 cups

This is quintessential Lake Creek Lodge fare and so easy to replicate. The lodge staff picked fresh mint from the banks of Lake Creek to create this sauce with an earthy sweetness. It's almost the same color and consistency of syrup, and we spooned it all over our lamb slices.

4 cups brown sugar

½ cup lemon juice

1 cup white vinegar

1 cup finely chopped fresh mint

Keep extra sauce in the refrigerator since it "lasts forever." For a smaller amount, cut the recipe in half but still use the full cup of mint.

Combine first three ingredients in a saucepan and bring to a simmer over medium heat. Continue to simmer about 15 minutes more, stirring occasionally, until mixture starts to thicken. (It will be runny, but it will thicken as it chills). Stir in the chopped mint.

Cool and refrigerate. Reheat gently before serving.

CURRIED RICE

Serves 4–6

This rice was always served with Roast Leg of Lamb (page 70), along with white rice for guests (and most of the kids) who preferred plain rice. The curry powder gives it a yellow color and adds a subtle, spicy flavor. The original recipe called for bacon grease, but olive oil works well as a substitute.

3 tablespoons olive oil

2 onions, finely chopped or grated

1 tablespoon curry powder

2 teaspoons sugar

2 teaspoons salt

2 teaspoons fresh lemon juice

1 cup dry white rice

Heat oil in a in frying pan over medium heat, add the onions, curry powder, sugar, salt and lemon juice. Cook, stirring frequently, until onions are translucent and cooked, about 5 minutes. Set aside.

Meanwhile, cook the rice according to package instructions until dry and fluffy. Mix rice into curry mixture, stirring and tossing lightly until well distributed (this can be done ahead of time and reheated in double boiler).

SAUTÉED CARROTS, CELERY & ONIONS

Serves 6–8

This was the era of overcooked vegetables which most of us are happy to leave behind. The kitchen served some straightforward vegetable sides, but there were very few actual recipes. Often the vegetable was just a supporting cast member to the bigger stars of the night, so they remain simple and unassuming.

1 tablespoons olive oil

6 carrots, peeled and cut diagonally into ½-inch-thick slices

4 ribs celery, cut diagonally into ½-inch-thick slices

1 onion, thinly sliced

1 tablespoon finely chopped fresh rosemary

salt and freshly ground black pepper

Heat the olive oil in a large (12-inch) sauté pan over medium heat, and add all of the vegetables and the rosemary. Season with salt and pepper and sauté for 7–8 minutes, stirring often to prevent over-browning, until the onions are translucent and the carrots are cooked but still a bit firm to the bite.

BLUEBERRY BUCKLE

Makes one 8 x 8-inch pan

One of Oregon's finest summertime crops is blueberries, and a visit to Lake Creek Lodge was (and still is), a good excuse to eat as many as possible. We'd spoon them over our cereal or have them in our pancakes in the morning, and hope for a special treat like this cake for dessert one night.

Batter:

> ½ cup (1 stick) butter, softened to room temperature
>
> ½ cup sugar
>
> 1 egg
>
> 2 cups flour
>
> 2 ½ teaspoons baking powder
>
> ¼ teaspoon salt
>
> ½ cup milk
>
> 2 cups fresh blueberries

Crumb Topping:

> ½ cup sugar
>
> ½ cup flour
>
> ½ teaspoon ground cinnamon
>
> ¼ cup butter, chilled and cut into 8 pieces

Preheat oven to 350°F. Line the bottom of an 8 x 8 x 2-inch pan with waxed paper.

In a mixer fitted with the paddle attachment, cream the butter and sugar until light and fluffy, about 3 minutes. Beat in the egg.

Sift together the flour, baking powder and salt. Add to the creamed mixture, alternating with the milk until it is all incorporated. Pour into the prepared pan and sprinkle the blueberries evenly over the top.

In a small bowl, mix the topping ingredients with fingertips until crumbly. Sprinkle over the berries.

Bake for 1 hour and 15 minutes, until a toothpick inserted into center comes out clean. Remove to a rack to cool.

Diana Pepperling serving guests in the buffet line

DAY 6

THURSDAY MENU

Cocktail Hour & Post-Dinner Hi Jinks

Sixty Minute Rolls

Corn Chowder

Honey-Mustard Glazed Ham

Raisin Sauce

Dijon Sauce

Scalloped Potatoes

Broccoli with Parmesan

Banana Cream Pie

Alternate Thursday Dinner Menu

Sixty Minute Rolls or Banana Bread

Lake Creek Lodge Salad

Roast Turkey

Cornbread Stuffing

Gravy

Mashed Potatoes

Broccoli with Parmesan

Chocolate Brownie Pie

AN IMPORTANT LAKE CREEK TRADITION WAS THE 6 P.M. cocktail hour. But this time of day wasn't always just for adults. After a long day of swimming, tennis, hiking, riding, fishing and biking, guests young and old would shower and dress for dinner about an hour before the dinner bell rang. Men combed their wet hair and put on fresh khakis and a collared shirt, women wore skirts, little girls wore sundresses, and little boys wore a collared shirt with their newly purchased Sisters cowboy boots.

Many guests become friends over their years of Lake Creek vacations. Before there were decks on cabins, guests would gather for cocktails on the lawn. Eventually, they'd gather on someone's cabin porch. This was arranged casually during the day, and one summer a group of families created a banner to hang on a cabin in the afternoon to indicate which family was hosting cocktail hour that night.

It was always bring-your-own-drink and the host would provide refills from a generously stocked bar, including soft drinks for kids, arranged on a porch table. Nobody had enough glasses for everyone, since the cabins were outfitted for one family, so guests simply walked over with their filled glass. They usually brought appetizers to share. And the hosting cabin would have an impressive spread of snacks. Cocktail hour fare was something we thought of during our packing at home (adding a can of smoked fish to our bags), or on our shopping trips to Sisters, but it wasn't fancy. Typical Lake Creek hors d'oeuvres included: layered bean dip, cashews, guacamole & chips, and smoked trout on crackers. This was a great time to get to know new guests who were invited over, and to exchange stories from the day. And cocktail hours were especially entertaining when outspoken Roblay presided over them. Toward the end of the hour, kids would run over to the lodge to make a line near the dinner bell. When Velda told them it was time, they'd take turns ringing the bell.

A young guest ringing the dinner bell

After a lively cocktail hour and even livelier dinner, hi-jinks would continue out by the pond. Horseshoes used to be a big part of Lake Creek Lodge, and there was a horseshoe pit on the lawn across from the lodge. Usually it was the dads who would gather there after dinner. We'd hear the clank of the metal horseshoes hitting the stake in the sand pit then roars of triumph or groans of despair as it grew darker outside.

Kids would sometimes go down the slide by the pond with their clothes on (much to their parents' chagrin). Dads might grab an unsuspecting pre-teen by the arms and legs, swing him back and forth by the edge of the pond's deep end…then into the pond!

The warm lodge was, and continues to be, a favorite place to relax after dinner. Most of us refined our competitive ping pong and pool table games at Lake Creek Lodge. And guests would talk, read magazines, organize bingo games (with candy prizes from Camp Sherman), and occasionally listen to talks by local residents.

Thursday was the only night with two different menus that were alternated each week, and one of those was a Thanksgiving menu. We never quite figured out why. According to a guest who worked as one of The Girls in the kitchen, the Raisin Sauce was gradually transferred to smaller saucepans as it reduced down to a sticky, syrupy consistency. For the designated "Pot Girl" in the kitchen, this meant extra pots added to the already large workload of keeping the kitchen clean before and after dinner service. Looking back at those chores the former kitchen girl remarked, "If we weren't cleaning the bloody raisin sauce pans, we were scrubbing the damn oven!" As for the pies, Roblay never served a pie with both a bottom and top crust — her fruit pies only had a top crust, and her cream pies only had a bottom crust.

SIXTY MINUTE ROLLS

Makes 2 dozen rolls

Crusty on the outside and soft on the inside, most of the summer these rolls were accompanied by orange marmalade or strawberry jam in small glass containers. Legend has it that every June a couple who came regularly to vacation at Lake Creek Lodge requested the rolls be served with apricot-pineapple jam and Roblay obliged. The original recipe yielded 8 dozen rolls, so just double or quadruple this scaled-down recipe for larger quantities.

1 cup milk

½ cup water

½ stick (¼ cup) butter

1 ½ cups flour, plus 1 ½ cups additional flour

2 tablespoons dry yeast

2 tablespoons sugar

1 teaspoon salt

Origin of the name? Perhaps because the dough needs to rise twice, for sixty minutes each time.

Combine milk, water and butter in a saucepan over low heat, and heat to 120–130°F; the butter does not need to melt.

Meanwhile, place 1 ½ cups flour, the yeast, sugar and salt in a mixing bowl. Gradually add the liquid mixture to the flour mixture and beat for 2 minutes on low speed. Add the remaining 1 ½ cups flour to make a soft dough, and beat 2 minutes on high speed. Scrape dough out onto a well-floured board, and blend to make a pliable dough. Set aside on the board covered loosely until doubled in size, about 1 hour.

Lightly oil two baking sheets. Shape dough into 24 rolls and place on baking sheets. Cover loosely and let rise another hour. Bake at 425°F for 12 minutes, swapping racks halfway for even browning. Remove from oven and transfer rolls to a rack to cool.

CORN CHOWDER

Serves 6–8

This is the original Lake Creek Lodge recipe, with some minor adjustments. Even though their version calls for canned corn, fresh corn would be a great substitute when at its peak in the middle of summer. For 3 cups of fresh corn kernels, you would need 5–6 ears of fresh corn. And you could thicken the soup by adding a cup of heavy cream in place of some of the milk in the recipe.

¼ pound bacon

1 onion, chopped

2 cups potatoes, peeled & diced
    (about 2 Yukon Gold potatoes)

3 cups boiling water

2 (15-ounce) cans sweet cream-style corn

¼ cup finely chopped pimento or red bell pepper

1 quart milk

2 teaspoons salt

¼ teaspoon freshly ground black pepper

1 teaspoon finely chopped fresh rosemary

½ cup shredded cheddar cheese

2 tablespoons minced fresh parsley

In a large saucepan, cook bacon over medium heat until browned and crisp, about 5 minutes. Remove bacon to drain on a plate lined with paper towels, and crumble when cool. Drain all but 1 tablespoon of the bacon drippings from the pan. Add the onion to the drippings in the pan and sauté over medium heat until soft, 3–5 minutes. Add the potatoes and water and simmer for 20 minutes, or until the potatoes are tender.

Add the corn, pimento, milk, salt, pepper, rosemary, and reserved bacon to pan. Heat slowly to a low simmer, stirring occasionally. Adjust the seasonings and serve hot with cheese & parsley sprinkled over the top of each bowl.

HONEY-MUSTARD GLAZED HAM

Serves 12–14

> 1 (12–14 pound) fully-cooked ham, trimmed of
>   excess rind and all but a ¼-inch layer of fat
>
> 1 cup honey
>
> ¼ cup grainy mustard
>
> ¼ cup packed dark brown sugar
>
> 2 tablespoons butter

Preheat oven to 350°F with rack in lower third of oven.

Score ham fat with a sharp knife in a diamond pattern without cutting into the meat. Place ham, cut side down, in a large roasting pan. Cover ham with parchment paper, then tightly cover roasting pan with foil. Bake for 1 ½–2 hours, depending on size of ham, to warm through.

Meanwhile, combine honey, mustard, sugar and butter in a small saucepan over medium-low heat until sugar dissolves, 3–5 minutes. Let glaze stand.

Remove ham from oven and discard foil and parchment. If there is no liquid in the roasting pan, add 1 cup of water to prevent glaze drippings from burning. Brush ham with half of honey-mustard glaze, return ham to oven and bake, uncovered, for 20–30 minutes. Brush with remaining glaze and bake until browned, about 20–30 more minutes.

Transfer ham to a cutting board and let rest for 15–20 minutes before carving.

RAISIN SAUCE

Makes about 1 ½ cups

　　¼ cup light brown sugar, firmly packed
　　1 tablespoon cornstarch
　　salt and freshly ground black pepper
　　1 cup apple cider
　　½ teaspoon ground mustard
　　¼ cup raisins
　　1 cinnamon stick
　　1 tablespoon butter

In a small saucepan over medium heat, combine all of the ingredients except the butter. Bring to a simmer and cook for 8–10 minutes, stirring often, until thickened. Remove from the heat and discard the cinnamon stick. Stir in the butter and serve warm.

DIJON SAUCE

Makes 2 cups

> 2 egg yolks
>
> 2 tablespoons Dijon mustard
>
> 2 tablespoons chopped shallots
>
> 1 teaspoon salt
>
> 1 teaspoon white pepper
>
> 1 ½ cups vegetable oil

Finely chopped onions can be substituted for the shallots, but the sauce won't hold up as long.

Combine all of ingredients except the oil in the bowl of a mixer and beat on high speed. Gradually add the oil and beat until combined.

SCALLOPED POTATOES

Serves 6

> 1 pound potatoes (about 6), such as Yukon Gold
> salt and freshly ground black pepper
> 3 tablespoons butter, cut into small cubes
> 2 ½ cups half-and-half or heavy cream

Preheat oven to 350°F. Generously butter a large gratin dish.

Peel and thinly slice the potatoes (a mandoline makes slicing easy). Layer potatoes in the prepared dish, overlapping slightly, and sprinkle each layer with some salt, pepper, and butter pieces. Pour the cream over the top, pressing down gently so the potatoes are submerged in the liquid.

Place in the oven and bake until top is browned and potatoes are tender, about 1 hour. Let stand 10 minutes before serving.

BROCCOLI WITH PARMESAN

Serves 6–8

Even though the lodge most likely served their broccoli plain, dressing up steamed broccoli with some olive oil and parmesan gives it a boost of flavor. But if you're serving this with a meal which already has complex flavors, sauces, or cheese, you might choose to omit the parmesan and serve the steamed broccoli on its own with a light drizzle of olive oil and some seasoning.

> 2 pounds broccoli (2–3 bunches), tough stems discarded
> 3 tablespoons olive oil
> ½ cup shredded Parmesan cheese
> salt and freshly ground black pepper

Cut broccoli into 2-inch wide florets.

Arrange a steamer rack over simmering water, place broccoli inside and steam, covered, until tender, about 5 minutes.

Transfer to a bowl and toss with the oil, cheese and salt and pepper to taste. Serve immediately.

BANANA CREAM PIE

Serves 8

The lodge version was simply their basic vanilla cream pie recipe, served with sliced bananas on top. Once chilled completely, this sweet pie keeps its shape beautifully when sliced and is refreshing on a hot day.

2/3 cup sugar

1/2 teaspoon salt

2 1/2 tablespoons cornstarch

1 tablespoon flour

3 cups whole milk

3 egg yolks, slightly beaten in a medium bowl

1 tablespoon butter, softened to room temperature

1 1/2 teaspoons vanilla

1 fully-baked single No-Fail Pie Crust (page 95)

2 ripe bananas for slicing on top

whipped cream (optional)

Have all of your ingredients prepped and ready before starting since the cream filling requires continual whisking in order to be successful.

Combine the sugar, salt, cornstarch and flour in a medium saucepan over moderate heat. Gradually add the milk, whisking constantly, until mixture thickens and begins to boil, about 5 minutes. Boil one minute longer, then remove from heat.

Slowly whisk half of the mixture into the egg yolks, then pour egg-milk mixture back into the saucepan. Return to moderate heat and boil for one minute, whisking constantly.

Remove from heat and whisk in the butter and vanilla.

Pour into the prepared pie crust and chill for at least 8 hours. Slice bananas over the top just before serving. Add a dollop of whipped cream if desired.

BANANA BREAD

Makes 1 loaf

Blanche's recipe yielded four loaves to feed a full house on the deck, but I reduced it down to one loaf. This bread is not quite as sweet as some banana breads, which makes it more appropriate at dinnertime.

> ½ cup shortening or butter, softened to room temperature
> 1 cup sugar
> 2 eggs, lightly beaten
> 1 teaspoon baking soda
> ½ cup milk
> 2 cups flour
> ⅛ teaspoon salt
> 2 ripe bananas, mashed

Preheat oven to 350°F. Grease a loaf pan.

Cream the shortening or butter with the sugar. Stir in eggs. Mix soda into milk, and add to mixture. Stir in flour, salt and bananas. Pour into prepared loaf pan and bake for 1 hour and 10 minutes, or until a wooden skewer comes out clean when inserted into the center. Cool for 30 minutes in the pan, then remove to a rack to cool completely.

ROAST TURKEY

Serves 10–12

Thanksgiving in July. It always seemed a bit funny to us kids to walk up to the buffet and be met with an entire Thanksgiving meal in the middle of summer. But we loved it all, and it was just one of those lodge traditions we grew to expect.

> 1 (12–14 pound) turkey, thawed completely
>   if previously frozen
> 2 tablespoons butter, melted
> salt and freshly ground black pepper

Remove turkey from refrigerator a half hour before roasting.

Preheat oven to 350°F, placing rack on lower third of oven.

Remove gizzards from neck or body cavity and place turkey, breast up, in a large roasting pan. Truss the legs together with kitchen string if desired. Brush turkey with butter, and sprinkle liberally all over outside and inside with salt and pepper.

Roast turkey, uncovered, until a meat thermometer inserted into the fleshiest part of the thigh registers about 165°F. If the pan smokes, pour a little stock or water into the bottom of the pan to keep the juices from burning. Total cooking time should be about 2 ½ –3 hours, depending on the size of the turkey.

When the bird is done, remove it from oven and tip so that the juices from the bird drain into the pan (save these for the gravy). Place turkey on a platter, cover with foil and let rest for a half hour before carving. (The internal temperature of the turkey will increase and the juices will set into the meat).

CORNBREAD STUFFING

Serves 10–12

Cornmeal was used often in lodge recipes, so it was natural for the kitchen to serve a cornbread-based stuffing alongside their turkey. The stuffing varied depending on who was making it that week, but these were the most common ingredients.

3 cups slightly dry bread cubes

5 cups coarsely crumbled cornbread

½ cup (1 stick) butter

1 onion, finely chopped

3 stalks celery, finely chopped (about 1 cup)

¼ cup chopped fresh parsley

½ teaspoon dried sage

½ teaspoon dried thyme

1 teaspoon salt

½ teaspoon freshly ground black pepper

2 eggs, beaten

¼ cup chicken broth or water

Stale bread works best.

Preheat oven to 375°F.

Toss together bread cubes and cornbread in a large bowl.

Melt the butter in a large skillet over medium heat, add the onion and celery, and sauté until tender but not brown, 3–5 minutes. Remove from heat and stir in parsley, sage, thyme, salt and pepper.

Pour vegetables and butter drippings over the bread, along with the eggs and broth. Toss lightly with a fork to coat the bread cubes. If the mixture seems too dry, add a little more broth.

Spoon mixture into a 9 x 13-inch casserole dish. Bake for 45 minutes, tossing every 15 minutes, until evenly browned.

CHOCOLATE BROWNIE PIE

Serves 8

This is a shallow pie, and not excessively dense or rich. The nuts are an important compliment to the chocolate brownie, and it's best served with a few spoonfuls of sweetened whipped cream or vanilla ice cream.

>   3 eggs
>   1 cup sugar
>   2 slices white bread (crusts removed),
>   crumbled, about ¾ cup
>   2 ounces (2 squares) unsweetened chocolate, melted
>   1 cup finely chopped nuts (walnuts or pecans)
>   1 partially baked single No-Fail Pie Crust (page 95)
>   whipped cream or vanilla ice cream

Preheat oven to 375°F.

Beat the eggs for 2 minutes on high speed, then reduce speed and gradually beat in the sugar. Crumble the bread and add to the egg mixture. Stir in the melted chocolate and nuts.

Pour mixture into the prepared pie shell and bake for 20 minutes. Cool pie before cutting, and serve with whipped cream or vanilla ice cream.

NO-FAIL PIE CRUST

Makes three 10-inch pie tops or bottoms

The lodge used lard, which makes for a flaky crust, but butter can be substituted for a rich, flavorful crust. The dough rolls out easily on a well-floured surface, and makes enough for several pies, so you could freeze some for another time.

> 2 ½ cups sifted flour
>
> 1 teaspoon salt
>
> 1 cup lard or butter (2 sticks), chilled &
> each stick cut into 12 pieces
>
> ¼ cup ice water
>
> 1 egg
>
> 1 tablespoon white vinegar

This pie dough can be made by hand in a bowl, using your fingertips to mix it lightly. A food processor makes it quick and easy as long as you don't over-process the dough.

Put the flour and salt in the bowl of a food processor fitted with the metal blade. Pulse a few times to combine. Add the lard or butter and pulse for 15 seconds, just until the mixture resembles coarse crumbs.

In a glass measuring cup, combine the water, egg and vinegar, and beat with a fork. Add to the flour mixture and pulse until flour is moistened and pastry forms into a ball.

Divide dough into thirds, place each onto a square of plastic wrap, press to form a 4-inch disk, and wrap tightly. Chill for at least 15 minutes or up to 3 days.

Place dough on a well-floured surface, sprinkle flour over the top, and roll the dough from the center out, lifting dough, turning it slightly, and occasionally flipping it over to keep it coated with flour. Roll dough to ⅛-inch thickness.

Line a pie pan with the dough, leaving about ¼-inch overhang, and flute the excess dough around the rim. Chill for 1 hour if pre-baking.

For a partially baked empty pie shell: Preheat oven to 375°F. Prick the sides and bottom of a chilled crust with a fork, line with foil and fill with dried beans to prevent crust from shrinking and bubbling. Bake for 15–20 minutes. Remove the foil and beans, and bake for another few minutes, until crust has a light golden color.

For a fully baked shell (in which the filling will require no additional baking and the pie will be chilled instead): Bake until crust is golden brown as above, adding another 10–15 minutes after removing the foil and beans.

28

DAY 7

FRIDAY MENU

Pitch Boats

Cinnamon Sticky Buns
Crunchy Cabbage Salad
Grilled Salmon with Tartar Sauce
Walla Walla Onion-Rice Casserole
Ice Cream Sundaes with Butterscotch Sauce
& "Lake Creek" Chocolate Sauce

FIRE AND WATER CAME TOGETHER AT LAKE CREEK LODGE every Friday night during the traditional pitch boat races. There was a lot of build-up to the evening's race, since families would spend the preceding days assembling their pitch boats.

Pitch boat building required two main elements: a piece of bark that would float, and enough pitch (sap), to burn for a long time. Early in the week, kids would go into the woods in search of a boat-worthy piece of bark. There were different styles of pitch-boat building, with some preferring a large piece of bark for a heavy vessel using weight for speed, and others opting for smaller rafts that might catch the wind. Once the bark was test-floated in the pond to make sure it was stable, it was usually set on top of a porch table where it would sit all week during the assembly process.

Kids often grabbed stainless steel spoons from their cabin's kitchen to go out and collect pitch during the day. This involved finding a tree that was oozing the amber-colored sap, and digging it out into a metal coffee container. It was not an easy task; the spoons usually bent, kids ended up with pitch in their hair and on their clothes, and everything they touched was sticky. But it was all for a very important cause.

Kids would pile the pitch onto their bark boat, sometimes using empty milk cartons as holding containers. Sticks made good masts for cardboard cereal box sails, and the fancier boats had flowers and leaves decorating them, along with small flags. Some with foresight, like teenage boys, brought firecrackers or sparklers on vacation with them and buried them in the pitch boats.

At the appointed hour after Friday's dinner, guests would gather in the dark alongside the pond. Kids would carefully transport their pitch boats to the grassy edge of the pond, usually using a team to gingerly carry their boats across the

lawn. Once the boats were assembled and admired, Glenna (and later Velda), would give the signal for the boats to be lowered into the water. In the early years, Al would douse the boats with kerosene or gasoline for extra flames. Glenna would then go along and light each boat and give it a push away from the bank, using a metal rake to keep the boats from floating too close to the edge and catching shrubbery on fire. It was quite a sight to stand at the edge of the pond, in the dark, with faces lit by the burning boats on the water. The natural current from the pond would encourage the boats to float across, but they'd be helped from the lifting of the wooden damn at the other end of the pond. And children would run around the pond attempting to propel boats with their waving arms and cheering voices. The first boat to reach the other side would win, and it would head down the creek with the other boats following. Perhaps to console the disappointed kids whose boats didn't win, Glenna and Velda would hand out fudgsicles and creamsicles to everyone.

In the beginning, management simply alerted the Forest Service each week about the pitch boat races so they wouldn't panic at the sight of black smoke rising from Lake Creek's property. Needless to say, after one dry summer and too many Oregon fires, the Forest Service put an end to the lighted pitch boats. But those of us who had grown up building pitch boats couldn't bear the thought of giving up the tradition. So we would continue to build the boats without the fire and float them across the pond unlit. They weren't as spectacular, but the kids still had fun. Since the pond is gone now, replaced by a curved stream with natural growth and logs, the environment is better suited for fish than for pitch boats. However some of the old time guests and their children are keeping the pitch boat tradition alive by sending the boats down the creek "rapids" for a distance, with the finish line at a designated spot near Cabin 11.

An especially beautiful pitch boat was on display for years in the lodge on the right side of the reception desk. It had a little cabin built atop a perfect piece of bark, and just the right amount of moss. It was too good to burn.

Since Friday night was usually the last night for most guests, there might be poems, awards or birthdays celebrated at dinner. One guest used to lead everyone in Cal cheers. Adults would bring over their leftover wine for dinner, and cocktail hour would be a buffet of whatever was left in the refrigerators. Thoughts of packing would be pushed to the last possible hour.

CINNAMON STICKY BUNS

Makes 30 buns

A favorite among guests, these sweet dinnertime treats disappeared quickly from their foil-lined bread baskets — especially at the kids' table where clever plots were hatched and carried out on unsuspecting new diners to secure additional buns. Since the buns preceded a big dinner, they were purposefully on the smaller side.

Dough:

> 1 teaspoon plus ¼ cup sugar
>
> 1 (¼-ounce) package active dry yeast
>
> ½ cup warm water
>
> ½ cup milk
>
> 4 tablespoons butter, cut into 8 pieces
>
> 1 teaspoon salt
>
> 2 eggs, beaten
>
> 4 cups all-purpose flour

Filling:

> ½ cup sugar
>
> 1 tablespoon cinnamon
>
> ½ cup chopped walnuts or pecans
>
> 2 tablespoons butter, melted

Topping:

> 1 cup brown sugar, firmly packed
>
> 4 tablespoons butter
>
> 3 tablespoons honey
>
> 1 tablespoon light corn syrup
>
> ½ cup chopped walnuts or pecans

Make the dough:

In a small bowl, dissolve 1 teaspoon of sugar and package of yeast in the warm water. Let stand until creamy, about 10 minutes. Meanwhile, warm the milk in a small saucepan until it bubbles, then remove from heat. Mix in the remaining ¼ cup sugar, butter and salt, and stir until melted. Let cool until lukewarm.

In the bowl of a mixer, combine the yeast mixture, the milk mixture, the eggs, and 1 ½ cups of the flour, and stir well to combine. Using a dough hook attachment if you have one, mix in the remaining 2 ½ cups of flour, ½ cup at a time, until dough pulls away from the sides of the bowl. Turn dough out onto a lightly floured board and knead for a few minutes until smooth and elastic.

Lightly oil a large bowl, place dough in the bowl and turn it to coat with oil. Leave seam side down, and cover with plastic wrap. Let rise at room temperature until doubled in volume, 1 to 2 hours.

While dough is rising, make the filling: Combine the sugar, cinnamon and nuts in a small bowl. Grease a 9 x 13-inch baking pan.

Turn the dough out onto a lightly floured surface, and roll into a 14 x 18-inch rectangle. Cut the rectangle in half lengthwise, creating two 7 x 18-inch rectangles. Brush the rectangles with the 2 tablespoons of melted butter, leaving ½-inch border. Sprinkle with the cinnamon-sugar mixture. Starting on the long side, lightly roll up each rectangle and pinch the seam to seal. Place seam side down and, using a serrated knife, cut into 15 pieces.

Make the topping: In a small saucepan over low heat, combine the sugar, butter, honey and corn syrup until sugar and butter are melted. Pour into the greased pan, and sprinkle with the nuts. Place the rolls cut side down in the prepared pan. Cover with plastic wrap and let rise for 1 hour until puffy. (Or cover tightly with plastic wrap, refrigerate overnight, and let stand at room temperature for 1 hour before baking).

Preheat oven to 375°F. Bake for 20–25 minutes, until golden brown and topping is bubbling. Let cool in pan for 3 minutes, then invert onto a serving platter.

These can be prepared in advance and refrigerated overnight before baking, which allows them to serve as a decadent breakfast treat as well.

CRUNCHY CABBAGE SALAD

Serves 6

This is a light and refreshing salad that first appeared on tables in the late 1970's. It uses packaged Ramen noodles which are best added just before serving so they stay crispy.

   ½ head cabbage, finely chopped

   2 teaspoons toasted sesame seeds

   ½ cup toasted slivered or sliced almonds

   4 green onions, chopped

   1 (3.1-ounce) package Ramen noodles, chicken flavored

Dressing:

   2 teaspoons sugar

   1 tablespoon vinegar

   ½ cup vegetable oil

   1 teaspoon salt

   ¼ teaspoon pepper

   1 packet Ramen chicken seasoning

Toss together first 4 salad ingredients. Crunch the dry noodles and add to the cabbage mix. (Reserve the seasoning packet for the dressing).

In a separate bowl, combine all the dressing ingredients.

Just before serving, add dressing to salad and toss well.

GRILLED SALMON WITH TARTAR SAUCE

Serves 4–6 (with extra sauce leftover)

Fresh salmon from the Pacific Northwest was, and still is, something to be savored. Bud cooked it on the open fire grills, a tradition followed for years.

Tartar Sauce:

 ½ cup mayonnaise

 1 tablespoon sweet or dill pickle relish

 1 tablespoon finely chopped shallots

 1 tablespoon drained capers

 2 teaspoons freshly squeezed lemon juice

 1 teaspoon Dijon mustard

 3 drops Tabasco sauce

Make the tartar sauce up to a day ahead and chill, covered, so the flavors can meld.

Salmon:

 1 (2-pound) salmon fillet, skin on

 olive oil

 salt and freshly ground black pepper

Prepare the sauce: Whisk all the ingredients together in a bowl. Cover and chill until ready to serve.

Heat a grill to medium-hot. Use a sharp knife to score the skin of the salmon in a shallow crosshatch pattern. Turn the fillet over and brush the top with olive oil and sprinkle with salt and pepper. Place the salmon on the grill skin side down, cover and cook for 8–10 minutes undisturbed. Remove with a large spatula and serve immediately with the Tartar Sauce.

WALLA WALLA ONION-RICE CASSEROLE

Serves 10

Lake Creek Lodge guest Sally Follen introduced this recipe to Blanche and her kitchen staff. It's great with any grilled foods, such as salmon, beef or lamb. If you can find them, use the large, sweet Walla Walla onions that are in season in the Northwest from June to September. Otherwise use another variety of mild white onion such as Vidalia. It's important to use Swiss cheese. The casserole improves in flavor if baked in advance. It may be refrigerated, then reheated.

> 4–5 Walla Walla sweet onions (about 3 pounds), thinly sliced or chopped
>
> 1 stick (½ cup) butter
>
> 1 cup uncooked white rice
>
> 1 ½ cups shredded Swiss cheese
>
> 1 ⅓ cups half & half
>
> salt and freshly ground black pepper

Preheat oven to 325°F. Grease a 9 x 13-inch casserole dish.

In a large pan, sauté the onions in butter until limp but not brown. Remove from heat.

Boil the rice in 2 cups of water for 5 minutes, then drain.

Mix together the onions, rice, cheese and half & half. Season with salt and pepper.

Bake, uncovered, for 1 hour.

ICE CREAM SUNDAES

The "ice cream sundae bar" evolved over time. In the early years, the staff brought out big cardboard tubs of ice cream — the kind used in ice cream parlors — and set them atop a wooden table on the buffet line. They scooped ice cream into our bowls and we ladled warm "Lake Creek" Chocolate Sauce or Butterscotch Sauce over the top, followed by whipped cream. Later on, Velda (who was always looking out for the kids' best interests), added bowls of festive toppings like gummy bears, chocolate jimmies and M&Ms. But the chocolate sauce was always the signature Lake Creek Lodge component that firmly anchored the dessert in tradition.

"Lake Creek" Chocolate Sauce (page 26)

Butterscotch Sauce (page 110)

whipped cream

toppings (toasted almonds, M&M's, chocolate jimmies, etc.)

tubs of ice cream

Pour the warm sauces into two different bowls and add small ladles. Set out whipped cream and bowls of toppings. Scoop ice cream for guests and let them help themselves to making their favorite sundae!

Velda with kids

BUTTERSCOTCH SAUCE

Makes 3 cups

For dessert some nights, Roblay would put out a big bowl of ice cream, accompanied by bowls of this butterscotch sauce, "Lake Creek" Chocolate Sauce, and fresh berries or sliced peaches. This is half of the lodge's original recipe, and it can be successfully halved again if desired.

> 1 cup Karo light corn syrup
> 1 ¾ cup light brown sugar
> 6 tablespoons butter
> pinch of salt
> 1 cup heavy cream

In a saucepan over low heat, melt the first four ingredients to the consistency of heavy syrup, whisking for 3–5 minutes. Remove from heat and let cool about 15 minutes. Gradually whisk in the cream.

Serve warm, or cover and refrigerate for up to a week.

DAY 8

BREAKFAST MENU

Departure

Lake Creek Lodge Raisin Bread
Buttermilk Pancakes
Cornmeal Battercakes
Sourdough Pancakes
Morning Glory Muffins
Old Fashioned Blueberry Muffins
Coffee Cake

BREAKFAST IN THE LODGE WAS NOT INCLUDED AS PART of the room & board at Lake Creek Lodge. But it was open to guests like a restaurant, with menus and wait staff. And for the guests in the original "hotel rooms" who didn't have kitchens, breakfast in the lodge was often a daily affair. It was a different experience from the nighttime dining since breakfast was, and still is, served indoors. It's a soothing atmosphere in the warm, knotty pine-walled dining room with the sun streaming in the paned windows and baking smells coming from the kitchen.

The old summer breakfast menu served the basics: eggs, bacon, hashed browns, hotcakes, homemade bread, French toast and stewed prunes. And the plate usually held a thick slice of sweet, ripe melon.

The Cornmeal Battercakes were Lake Creek Lodge's signature pancakes served at breakfast, and they had a distinctive grainy texture from the cornmeal. Buttermilk Pancakes were an alternative, and Diana was told by one customer that they were the "best hotcakes west of the Mississippi." For toast, the kitchen used whatever homemade bread they had on hand (usually the Easy French Bread, Lake Creek Lodge Raisin Bread, or a homemade wheat bread). A favorite with the kids was toasted raisin bread sprinkled with cinnamon-sugar.

The breakfast menu now is more extensive, and a coffee bar was added to the lodge so guests can order lattes and warm drinks in the morning. One recent chef successfully asked a local coffee company to create "Roblay's Blend" coffee beans for Lake Creek Lodge. Over the years the lodge has also added muffins, coffee cakes, marionberry pancakes, eggs benedict and breakfast breads to the menu.

Breakfast in the lodge was often part of the routine of departure day. Luggage was packed, cars were filled and the kitchens were cleared out. Families could prolong the vacation a bit and enjoy one more meal before embarking on the drive home. This was a last chance to say goodbye to friends and staff, soak up the beauty of Lake Creek Lodge and linger for a few more moments over the hearty lodge cooking.

LAKE CREEK LODGE RAISIN BREAD

Makes 2 loaves

The kitchen added a "handful of raisins" to their basic bread batter to create the heavenly raisin bread. I translated that to a cup of raisins for every loaf of bread, but you can adjust as you please. For breakfast, we ate raisin bread toasted with melted butter running down our chins.

> 1 tablespoon dry yeast
>
> ½ cup warm water
>
> 1 ½ tablespoons sugar
>
> 6 cups all purpose flour, divided in half
>
> 1 teaspoon salt
>
> 2 cups warm water
>
> 2 cups raisins

In the bowl of a mixer, dissolve yeast in ½ cup warm water (100°–110°F), and let sit for 10 minutes. Stir in the sugar. Add 3 cups of the flour and the salt to the yeast mixture to make a thick, crumbly paste. Add the 2 cups warm water and beat until batter is smooth. Mix in the raisins. Then add the remaining 3 cups of flour. The dough will be sticky.

Scrape the dough onto a well-floured work surface, sprinkle the top with flour, and knead for two minutes. Form a smooth, round ball of dough. Oil a large bowl, add the dough, and cover with plastic wrap. Let it rise so it doubles in bulk, 2 hours.

Grease two loaf pans. Divide dough in half and fill each loaf pan. Cover loaves loosely with a towel and allow to rise until doubled and light, about 1 hour.

Preheat oven to 350°F. Bake loaves for 1 hour, or until done. Remove from oven and turn onto rack to cool.

BUTTERMILK PANCAKES

Serves 4 (Makes about 16 pancakes)

Standard lodge fare, these arrived at the table in steaming stacks. Sometimes we were offered fresh blueberry pancakes as a variation. After pouring batter into the pan, sprinkle blueberries over the pancake, then flip when ready and finish cooking.

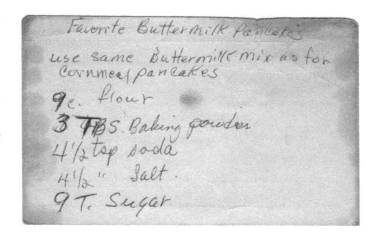

2 eggs

2 cups buttermilk

3 tablespoons oil

1 ½ cups flour

1 tablespoon sugar

2 teaspoons baking powder

1 teaspoon baking soda

½ teaspoon salt

Beat together the eggs, buttermilk and oil, and set aside.

Sift together the flour, sugar, baking powder, baking soda, and salt. Stir in the wet ingredients.

Pour about ¼ cup batter into a greased skillet for each pancake.

Serve warm with syrup.

CORNMEAL BATTERCAKES

Serves 4 (Makes about 16 pancakes)

While testing this pancake recipe, the kitchen filled with the warm, nutty smells of cornmeal — reminders of relaxed summer breakfasts in the lodge. The cornmeal gives the pancakes a hearty texture, and pairs beautifully with warm syrup.

2 eggs
2 cups buttermilk
3 tablespoons oil
½ cup flour
1 teaspoon baking soda
½ teaspoon salt
1 cup cornmeal

Beat together the eggs, buttermilk and oil, and set aside.

Sift together the flour and baking soda, then stir in the salt and cornmeal until just mixed. Stir in the wet ingredients.

Pour about ¼ cup batter into a greased skillet for each pancake.

Serve warm with syrup.

SOURDOUGH PANCAKES

Serves 4 (Makes about 16 pancakes)

These are thinner pancakes and very easy to flip. Make the starter the night before, and it will begin the fermentation process to give the pancakes that unique sourdough flavor. Then just add the remaining ingredients in the morning.

Basic Starter:

> 2 cups flour
> 2 cups water

Pancake Mix:

> 1 egg
> 1 teaspoon baking soda
> 1 teaspoon salt
> 1 tablespoon sugar
> 2 tablespoons vegetable oil

Make the Basic Starter by mixing the flour and water in a bowl and letting it sit at room temperature overnight.

To the 4 cups of Basic Starter, add the egg, baking soda, salt, sugar and oil and stir to combine.

Pour about ¼ cup batter into a greased skillet for each pancake.

Serve warm with syrup.

MORNING GLORY MUFFINS

Makes 16 muffins

These muffins were a favorite of Roblay's. They are hearty and moist without being overly sweet. Glenna, the longtime manager, used to bake a batch every week and Roblay would have one in the morning along with half a banana and half an apple. She usually ate the top off the muffin and gave the rest to her dog Daisy.

2 cups flour

2 teaspoons ground cinnamon

2 teaspoons baking soda

½ teaspoon salt

1 ¼ cups sugar

1 ½ cups finely shredded carrots (3 large carrots)

2 large tart apples, peeled and shredded

½ cup raisins (optional)

¾ cup shredded coconut

½ cup chopped pecans or walnuts

3 eggs, lightly beaten

1 cup vegetable oil

½ teaspoon vanilla

Preheat oven to 375°F. Grease the muffin tins.

Sift flour with cinnamon, baking soda and salt into a large bowl. Stir in sugar until blended. Add carrots, apples, raisins, coconut and nuts, and blend well. Make a well in the center of mixture and pour in eggs, oil & vanilla. Stir until evenly mixed. Fill muffin tins ¾ way full.

Bake for 20 minutes, or until a toothpick inserted into the center of a muffin comes out clean. Remove muffins from tins to cool on a rack.

Roblay (in foreground) hiking with friends

OLD FASHIONED BLUEBERRY MUFFINS

Makes 12 muffins

These light, flavorful muffins are quick and easy to prepare. The lodge recipe notes say orange zest can be used in place of lemon zest, and unthawed frozen blueberries in place of fresh blueberries during the winter months.

2 cups flour

½ cup sugar

1 tablespoon baking powder

½ teaspoon salt

1 teaspoon grated lemon zest

1 cup fresh blueberries

¾ cup milk

⅓ cup vegetable oil

1 egg

Preheat oven to 400°F. Grease bottoms only of muffin tin.

In a medium bowl, combine flour, sugar, baking powder, salt and lemon zest with a fork. Stir in blueberries. In a small bowl, combine milk, oil and egg. Add to dry ingredients and stir just until dry ingredients are moistened.

Fill muffin cups ⅔ full. Bake 20 minutes, until light brown. Remove muffins from tin to cool on a rack.

COFFEE CAKE

Serves 8–10

This is an unusual coffee cake in that the topping is spread across the bottom of the pan, the batter is baked on top, then the whole cake is inverted. The result is a light cake with a caramel-nut coating. It's best served warm, but holds well for a day wrapped airtight.

  1 cup sour cream
  2 eggs
  ½ teaspoon baking soda
  1 ½ cups bread flour
  1 cup sugar
  2 teaspoons baking powder
  ¼ teaspoon salt

Topping:

  ¾ cup light brown sugar
  2 tablespoons butter, melted
  1 tablespoon cream
  ¾ cup chopped walnuts

Preheat oven to 350°F. Grease a 9 x 9-inch pan with butter.

Beat together the sour cream, eggs and baking soda in a large bowl. Sift the flour, sugar, baking powder and salt in a separate bowl. Add dry ingredients to sour cream mixture and mix until smooth.

Line the pan with the brown sugar. Drizzle with the melted butter and cream, stir to combine, add the nuts and spread over the bottom of pan. Pour the batter over the nut mixture, gently evening it out with the spoon. Bake 30–35 minutes. Cool on a rack for 5 minutes, then invert onto rack to cool before slicing.

CONCLUSION

AFTER BREAKFAST, WE WOULD PAY OUR BILL AND try to avoid the truth that our Lake Creek vacation had come to an end. We had hiked mountains, won tennis games, run through the woods, read on our porches, biked to Camp Sherman, played rounds of ping pong, and enjoyed hearty meals as we deepened our Lake Creek friendships.

We loaded our cars and gathered on the lawn in front of the cabins for last farewells and promises to see each other the following summer. Sometimes we'd bottle a bit of the ice cold "Lake Creek Water" to drink at home, or tuck a piece of bright green moss into our bag to remind us of our glorious week. It was a sad time to slowly pull out of the driveway, gravel crunching under the tires. We'd drive away waving and honking, looking back, and sometimes making one last trip to Camp Sherman to stock up on penny candy for the long ride home.

Lake Creek Lodge is now a year-round resort and the cabins have been winterized. A group of us were overcome with enthusiasm as we checked out last August, unable to completely say goodbye for a full year, and so we booked a New Year's Eve reunion. Some of us had never experienced Lake Creek Lodge in the winter, and the thought of returning again soon made our summer parting a little easier.

So now we're settled into cozy cabins with colorful lights and a fire roaring in the lodge fireplace. A fresh blanket of snow has covered the ground and dusted the trees and bushes white. It's a magical setting with the snow sparkling in the moonlight. The air is cold, but the creek is still flowing and we're anticipating a festive New Year's dinner in the lodge. The lodge food will undoubtedly be good. But most importantly, the cabin guests will gather together. The scene outside is much different from summer. But inside we'll be sharing a dinner in our beloved lodge, happy to start another year surrounded by Lake Creek friends and the promise of many more summers and meals together at this little Oregon resort.

Roblay McMullin

Margaret Lumpkin (left) & Velda Brust (right)

Gordon & Jeff Jones

INDEX

ACKNOWLEDGMENTS

Completed over several summer visits, this book is for all the loyal Lake Creek Lodge guests and staff who have worked to keep the history alive. Special thanks to:

- ❀ Sally Follen for her longstanding love of Lake Creek Lodge and the stories she tells stretching back to her youth — all with a twinkle in her eye, a sense of humor, and boundless enthusiasm.

- ❀ Diana Pepperling for filling in the blanks when recipes had no directions, and recounting stories about Walker's baking escapades.

- ❀ Kathleen Follen for her valuable collaboration, memories and creativity.

- ❀ Gordon and Jeff Jones, and the lodge staff, for generously allowing us access to old photographs and for keeping the resort going for future generations.

- ❀ Shannon Bodie for capturing the spirit of the resort in her design and layout, and confidently guiding the book through the publishing process.

- ❀ My parents, Tim and Annette Ryan, who made their first trip from California to Lake Creek Lodge almost 50 years ago on the recommendation of Peter and Joan Avenali.

- ❀ My siblings Matt, Kelley and Kate for sharing the back seat, remembering the horses' names and continuing the traditions with our own kids.

- ❀ My husband John, for wholeheartedly embracing Lake Creek Lodge, and our children Lucy, Henry and Charlie for tasting recipes, wise editing, patience when I missed a hike because of "the cookbook," and their devotion to our family adventures.

ABOUT THE AUTHOR

ONE OF FOUR RYAN CHILDREN, JULI TANTUM GREW UP going to Lake Creek Lodge in the way back of the family station wagon. As a freelance food writer, she has worked in test kitchens and assisted with several cookbooks. Her recipes and writing have appeared in the food sections of the *Los Angeles Times* and the *Chicago Tribune*, and also on the *TV Food Network*. Juli is a graduate of Brown University and the California Culinary Academy. She lives outside of San Francisco with her husband and three kids, and now rides up to Oregon in the front seat.